The Crucible of Light

Additional Titles by Dr. Javad Nurbakhsh

1. The Path: Sufi Practices
2. Masters of the Path
3. Sufi Women
4. Divani Nurbakhsh: Sufi Poetry
5. Traditions of the Prophet, Vol. I
6. Traditions of the Prophet, Vol. II
7. Sufism I: Meaning, Knowledge and Unity
8. Sufism II: Fear and Hope, Contraction and Expansion, Gathering and Dispersion, Intoxication and Sobriety, Annihilation and Subsistence
9. Sufism III: Submission, Contentment, Absence, Presence, Intimacy, Awe, Tranquillity, Serenity, Fluctuation, Stability
10. Sufism IV: Repentance, Abstinence, Renunciation, Wariness, Humility, Humbleness, Sincerity, Constancy, Courtesy
11. Sufism V: Gratitude, Patience, Trust-in God, Aspiration, Veracity, Zeal, Valour, Altruism, Shame
12. Jesus in the Eyes of the Sufis
13. Spiritual Poverty in Sufism
14. The Great Satan, "Eblis"
15. Sufi Symbolism I: Parts of the Beloved's Body; and Wine, Music, Audition and Convivial Gatherings
16. Sufi Symbolism II: Love, Lover, Beloved, Allusions and Metaphors
17. Sufi Symbolism III: Religious Terminology
18. Sufi Symbolism IV: Symbolism of the Natural World
19. Sufi Symbolism V: Veils and Clothing, Government, Economics and Commerce, Medicine and Healing
20. Sufi Symbolism VI: Titles and Epithets
21. Sufi Symbolism VII: Contemplative Disciplines, Visions and Theophanies, Family Relationships, Servants of God, Names of Sufi Orders
22. Sufi Symbloism VIII: Inspirations, Revelations, Lights; Charismatic Powers; Spiritual States and Stations; Praise and Condemnation
23. Sufi Symbolism IX: Spiritual Faculties, Spiritual Organs, Knowledge, Gnosis, Wisdom and Perfection
24. Sufi Symbolism X: Spiritual States and Mystical Stations
25. Sufi Symbolism XI: Spiritual States and Mystical Stations
26. Sufi Symbolism XII: Spiritual States and Mystical Stations
27. Sufi Symbolism XIII: Scribes, Pens, Tablets, Koranic Letters, Words, Discourse, Speech, Divine Names, Attributes and Essence
28. Sufi Symbolism XIV: The Unity of Being
29. Sufi Symbolism XV: Reality, the Divine Attributes and the Sufi Path
30. Sufi Symbolism XVI: Index
31. Discourses on the Sufi Path
32. Dogs from the Sufi Point of View
33. Psychology of Sufism (*Del wa nafs*)
34. The Truths of Love: Sufi Poetry

The Crucible of Light

Sufi Terms Illuminated

Dr. Javad Nurbakhsh

KHANIQAHI NIMATULLAHI PUBLICATIONS

NEW YORK LONDON

www.nimatullahi.org

Library of Congress Cataloging-in-Publication Data

Nurbakhsh, Javad.
[Kashkul-i nur. English]
The crucible of light : Sufi terms illuminated / Javad Nurbakhsh. -- 1st ed.
p. cm.
Includes index.
ISBN 978-0-933546-82-0 (pbk. : alk. paper)
1. Sufism--Terminology. I. Title.
BP188.48.N87413 2009
297.403--dc22

2009013074

Printed in the United States of America

Translated by Terry Graham and Jawid Mojaddedi
Cover photo provided by Hessink's Auctions, The Netherlands
Cover design and layout by Lolo Saney

Contents

Preface 15
Foreword 17
Note on the Translation 19
Table of Transliteration Equivalents 21

Sincerity (*ikhlāṣ*) 23
The Ethics of the Sufis (*akhlāq-i ṣūfiyān*) 25
Etiquette (*adab*) 30
Devotion (*irādat*) 31
Marriage (*izdiwāj*) 32
Guide or Master (*ustād yā pīr*) 33
Seeking Forgiveness (*istighfār*) 36
Constancy (*istiqāmat*) 36
Submission (*islām*) 37
Allusion and Expression (*ishārat wa ʿibārat*) 38
God is Greater! (*Allāhu akbar!*) 38
Absolute Divinity (*Ulūhiyyāt*) 39
Commanding Right and Forbidding Wrong (*amr bi-maʿrūf wa nahī az munkar*) 40
"I am the Truth" ("*anā l-Ḥaqq*") 40
Intimacy (*uns*) 41
The People on the Mystical Path to God (*ahl-i ṭarīq-i Allāh*) 43

Favoring of Others (*īthār*) 44
Faith and Unbelief (*īmān wa kufr*) and Believer and Unbeliever (*mu'min wa kāfir*) 46
The Idol (*but*) 47
The Worst of Times (*badtarīn rūzigār*) 48
Staring at Others (*bisyār nigarīstan bi dīgarān*) 48
Devoteeship (*bandagī* or *'ubūdiyat*) 48
Heaven and Hell (*bihisht wa dūzakh*) 51
Practice of Poverty (*parsa*) 54
Detachment from the World (*tajrīd*) 55
Fear (*tars*) 56
Sufism (*taṣawwuf*), the Sufi (*ṣūfī*), the Sufiologist (*mutaṣawwif*), the Dervish (*darwish*) and Dervishness (*darwīshī*) 56
Exegesis or Interpretation (*tafsīr*) 77
Reflection (*tafakkur* or *fikr*) 78
Piety (*taqwā*) 80
Magnification [of God's Name] (*takbīr*) 81
Fluctuation (*talwīn*), Stability (*tamkīn*), Extinction (*iṣṭilām*) and Effacement (*maḥw*) 82
Would-be Ecstasy (*tawājud*), Ecstasy (*wajd*) and True Being (*wujūd*) 83
Humility (*tawāḍu'*) 85
Repentance (*tawba*) 85
Adherence to Divine Unity (*tawḥīd*) and the Adherent to Divine Unity (*muwaḥḥid*) 88
Unity (*tawḥīd*), its Affirmer (*muwaḥḥid*) and the Object of Affirmation (*muwaḥḥad*) 92

The Unity of God (*tawḥīd-i Ḥaqq*) and the Unity of Creation (*tawḥīd-i khalq*)	93
Trust-in-God (*tawakkul*), Submission (*taslīm*) and Consignment (*tafwiḍ*)	93
Making Accusations (*tuhmat*)	97
Ambition (*jāh-ṭalabī*)	97
Determinism and Free Will (*jabr wa ikhtiyār*)	98
Concentration and Dispersion (*jam*ʿ *wa tafriqa*)	99
Chivalry (*jawānmardī* or *futuwwat*)	102
Generosity (*jūd*), Liberality (*sakhā*) and Meanness (*bukhl*)	109
Need (*ḥājat*)	110
State and Station (*ḥāl wa maqām*)	111
The Pilgrimage and Visitation of the Kaʿba (*ḥājj wa ziyārat-i kaʿba*)	112
Veil (*ḥijāb*)	119
Freedom (*ḥurriyat*)	120
Presence and Absence (*ḥuḍūr wa ghaybat*)	121
God or the Truth (*Ḥaqq*)	123
Truth and Falsity (*ḥaqq wa bāṭil*)	125
Wisdom (*ḥikmat*)	126
Shame (*ḥayā*)	128
Eternal Life (*ḥayāt-i abad*)	128
Perplexity (*ḥayrat*) and Bewilderment (*taḥayyur*)	129
Silence (*khāmūshī*)	129
God-cognition (*khudā-shināsī*)	131
Service (*khidmat bi-khalq*)	133
Submissiveness (*khushū*ʿ)	135
Temperament (*khulq*)	136
People (*khalq*)	138

Retreat and Seclusion (*khalwat wa ʿuzlat*) 139
Passing Thoughts (*khawāṭir*) 141
Fear and Hope (*khawf wa rajā*) 143
Supplicatory Prayer (*duʿā*) 145
The Heart (*dil*) 147
The World and the Hereafter (*dunyā wa ākhirat*) 148
Fortune (*dawlat*) 151
Remembrance (*dhikr*) 151
Savor and Imbibing (*dhawq wa shurb*) 154
The Path of God (*rāh-i Ḥaqq*) 156
Mercy (*raḥmat*) 157
Contentment (*riḍā*) 158
The Heart-based Soul (*rūʿ*) 161
Hypocrisy (*riyā*) 161
Ascetic Discipline (*riyāḍat*) 162
Asceticism (*zuhd*) and the Ascetic (*zāhid*) 163
Intoxication and Sobriety (*sukr wa ṣaḥw*) 165
Audition and Ecstasy (*samāʿ wa wajd*) 167
Joy and Sorrow (*shādī wa andūh*) 169
Evil (*sharr*) and the Ultimate Evil (*sharr-i sharr*) 170
The Law (*sharīʿat*), the Path (*ṭarīqat*) and Reality (*ḥaqīqat*) 171
Kindness towards Others (*shafaqat bar khalq*) 172
Thanks (*shukr*) 173
Recognition of the Divine Unity of Being (*shinākht-i tawḥīd-i wujūd*) 174
Yearning (*shawq*) 176
Lust (*shahwat*) 177
The Preacher (*wāʿi*) 177
Patience (*ṣabr*) 179

Association (*ṣuḥbat*) 182
Veracity (*ṣidq*) 183
The *Ṣirāṭ* Bridge (*ṣirāṭ*) 184
Devotional Practice (*ṭāʿat*) 185
Seeking the Way (*ṭalab-i ṭarīq*) and Seeking God (*ṭalab-i Ḥaqq*) 187
Seeking (*ṭalab*), Finding (*yāft*) and Witnessing (*mushāhada*) 187
Greed (*ṭamaʿ*) 189
The Gnostic (*ʿārif*) 189
Worship (*ʿibādat*) and the Worshipper (*ʿābid*) 194
Seclusion (*ʿuzlat*) 195
Love (*ʿishq*) 195
God's Bestowal (*ʿaṭā-yi Khudāwand*) 198
Intellect (*ʿaql*) and the Reasoner (*ʿāqil*) 198
Reason and Love (*ʿaql wa ʿishq*) 199
Reprisal (*ʿuqūbat*) 208
Knowledge (*ʿilm*) and the Knower (*ʿālim*) 209
Festival (*ʿīd*) 215
The Vision of Certitude (*ʿayn al-yaqīn*), the Knowledge of Certitude (*ʿilm al-yaqīn*) and the Truth of Certitude (*ḥaqq al-yaqīn*) 215
Alienation (*ghurbat*) 216
Overwhelmings (*ghalabāt*) 217
Gossip (*ghaybat*) 218
Jealousy-in-Love (*ghayrat*) 219
Heart-discernment (*firāsat*) 220
Singularity (*fardāniyyat*) 222
Obligatory Practice (*farīḍa*) and Customary Practice (*sunnat*) 223
Poverty (*faqr*) and the Pauper (*faqīr*) 223

Annihilation and Subsistence (*fanā wa baqā*) 225
Contraction and Expansion (*qabḍ wa basṭ*) 229
Contentment-with-Sufficiency (*qanā'at*) 231
Cardinal Sins (*kabā'ir*) 233
Pride (*kibr*) 234
Livelihood (*kasb*) 234
The Sufis' Clothing (*libās-i ṣūfiyān*) 235
Luminous Manifestation (*lawā'iḥ*), Effulgence (*lawāmi'*) and Auroral Illumination (*ṭawāli'*) 235
Loving-kindness (*maḥabbat*) and Friendship (*dūstī*) 237
The Claimant (*mudda'ī*) 242
Meditation (*murāqaba*) and Attention (*tawajjuh*) 243
The Patched Cloak (*muraqqa'*) and the Water-skin (*rakwa*) 244
Humanity (*muruwwat*) 246
The Disciple (*murīd*) and the Master (*murād*) 247
Muslim-ness (*musalmānī*) and the Muslim (*musalmān*) 248
Witnessing (*mushāhada*), Visionary Revelation (*mukāshafa*) and Presential Vision (*muḥāḍara*) 249
The Polytheist (*mushrik*) 251
Gnosis (*ma'rifat-i Ḥaqq*) 252
Transgression (*ma'ṣiyat*) 255
Deception (*makr*) 256
Incurring Blame (*malāmat*) 256
'I and You' ('*man wa tu*') 257
Harmony (*muwāfaqat*) 261
The Self (*nafs*) 262
Daily Prayers (*namāz*) and Fasting (*rūza*) 266
Need (*niyāz*) and Freedom from Need (*bī-niyāzī*) 269
The Intermediary (*wāsiṭa*) 272

The One Who Has Reached Union (*wāṣil*) 273
Being (*wujūd*) and Nothingness (*ʿadam*) 273
Oneness (*Waḥdāniyyat*) 274
Litany (*wird*) 275
Litany on the Tongue (*wird-i zabān*) and Remembrance in the Soul (*dhikr-i jān*) 275
Abstinence (*waraʿ*) 276
Temptation (*waswasa*) and Inspiration (*ilhām*) 277
Fidelity (*wafā*) 277
The Moment (*waqt*) 278
The Friend of God (*walī*) and Friendship with God (*walāyat*) 280
Aspiration (*himmat*) 281
Identity (*huwiyyat*) 282
Awe (*haybat*) and Intimacy (*uns*) 283
Certitude (*yaqīn*) 283

List of Sources 285
Index of Terms 287

In the name of Absolute Being

Preface

Over the years that I have studied the sayings of the Masters of the Path, whenever an interesting explanation caught my attention I would make a note of it. A few years ago it occurred to me that I should gather these quotations into a book to be published under the title *The Crucible of Light.*

A sincere devotee who is constantly committed with ardent zeal to the duties of the *khānaqāh* (Sufi center) suggested to me that under each heading I should also give a definition of my own. I have done so accordingly, putting asterisks after each definition of mine, followed by the definitions I have culled from masters of the past. Now, this new edition of *The Crucible of Light*, which has additional terms I have included, can be considered a supplement to the *Sufi Symbolism* series.

May this book be of interest to those who have the appropriate perception.

—Dr. Javad Nurbakhsh
November 2005

Foreword

The Crucible of Light was first published in Persian under the title of *Kashkul-e Nur* in 2001, some seven years before my father's passing away. He intended it to be a supplement to his 16 volume *Encyclopedia of Sufi Symbolism.*

My father, Dr. Javad Nurbakhsh, wrote prolifically on the subject of Sufism, and his books, in the main, consist of compilations of classical Sufi texts for the purpose of explaining Sufi terms. For him classical Sufi texts, written from the 9th to the 14th centuries A.D. were the key to 'understanding' Sufi concepts, though he was always quick to point out that, in truth, Sufism can only be understood by those who embark on the Spiritual Path.

In his *Encyclopedia of Sufi Symbolism*, my father rarely found it necessary to express his own ideas about Sufism. Perhaps this was because he believed that Sufi terms have been sufficiently well explained and clarified by the classical Sufi authors and, therefore, there is no purpose in reiterating what others have already stated so eloquently. In *The Crucible of Light*, as he himself writes in the preface, he was asked by one of his disciples to give his own explanation of Sufi terms under each entry. This, in fact, may be the only reason why he did so.

My father's entries in this book are short and to the point. Often, they are an endorsement of the points of view of the Sufi authors that he quotes. Readers will notice, I trust, that there is one theme running through all his contributions: the negation of self as a way to reach God. He defines a 'Sufi' as one who is liberated from himself/herself, who has become joined to God. He further defines 'hell' as the world of ego, 'heaven' as liberation from such a world, and 'humility' as being nothing when dealing with people in the world, an attribute he himself embodied all of his life.

—Dr. Alireza Nurbakhsh
April 2009

Note on the Translation

In the Persian language third person singular pronouns have no gender. Thus, there is no distinction between 'he' and 'she' or 'him' and 'her' or 'his' and 'her'. In this translation the masculine form of the pronoun has been used throughout the text in order to avoid the awkwardness of repeating, for example, 'him or her'. This has been done without any intent to suggest that the masculine is preferable or more applicable to the subject matter of any passage than the feminine. Indeed, Sufism makes no distinction between men and women in travelling the path to God.

Persian and Arabic words used in the original Persian text of this book have been transliterated in this English edition using the transliteration equivalents set forth on page 21. However, certain terms that are commonly used in English, such as 'shaikh', 'dervish' and 'jinn', are set forth using one of their commonly accepted English spellings.

Certain transliterated terms are used throughout the book without separate definition because they are discussed in specific sections of the text. Thus, the word '*dhikr*', which literally means 'remembrance' and refers to the sufi practice of the selfless remembrance of God, is discussed at pages 151-154; and the word *'nafs'*, which is commonly translated as the 'ego', or 'lower self', is discussed at pages 262-266.

The terms discussed in this book are arranged in accordance with the original Persian text, which employed an alphabetical arrangement based on the Persian alphabet. An index is provided on pages 287-292, with the terms listed alphabetically according to their English translations.

Each quoted prose passage in the book is followed by a citation, set forth in parentheses, indicating by a designated abbreviation the source of the quotation. These abbreviations, together with the names of the classical Sufi texts to which they refer, are set forth on pages 285-286.

Each quoted poetic passage in the book is followed by the poet's name when the source is a poet's collection (e.g. 'Ḥafiz' for *Dīwān-i Ḥafiz*; Rūmī for *Dīwān-i Shams-i Tabrizī*), and by the name of the work when the source is a single poem, such as Rūmī's poem, the *Mathnawī*.

Table of Transliteration Equivalents

PERSIAN ARABIC	LATIN	PERSIAN ARABIC	LATIN
CONSONANTS			
ء	ʾ	ض	ḍ
ب	b	ط	ṭ
ت	t	ظ	ẓ
ث	th	ع	ʿ
ج	j	غ	gh
ح	ḥ	ف	f
خ	kh	ق	q
د	d	ك	k
ذ	dh	ل	l
ر	r	م	m
ز	z	ن	n
س	s	و	w
ش	sh	ه	h
ص	ṣ	ي	y
		ة	a

PERSIAN ARABIC	LATIN
LONG VOWELS	
آ	ā
أُو	ū
اِي	ī
SHORT VOWELS	
َ	a
ُ	u
ِ	i
DIPTHONGS	
أَو	aw
أَي	ay
PERSIAN CONSONANTS	
پ	p
ژ	zh
چ	ch
گ	g

In the Name of God

Sincerity (*ikhlāṣ*)

Author: The sincerity of the sufi is thinking only of God. Veracity precedes sincerity, which begins only after one engages in practice.

There are three types of sincerity:

1. Sincerity with people, which means not to do things simply for appearances in one's dealings and associations with others.
2. Sincerity with the master or beloved, which means having upright thoughts and actions both outwardly and inwardly.
3. Sincerity with God, which means never forgetting God and making sure that everything one says and does is for the sake of His satisfaction and in service to Him.

***

Ruwaym: Sincerity in practice is to expect nothing from the two worlds in return for one's efforts. (TA 486)

Kharaqānī: Whatever you do for the sake of God is sincerity, and whatever you do for the sake of the creation is hypocrisy. (TA 701)

Abū Yaʿqūb Sūsī: Whoever sees sincerity in his own sincerity is in need of further sincerity. (RQ 324)

Ad-Daqqāq: Sincerity is to keep oneself from being observed by people. Veracity (*ṣidq*) is to resist following one's *nafs*. The sincere one is without ostentation; the veracious one is free from self-conceit. (RQ 323)

Abū ʿUthmān Maghribī: Sincerity is something in which your *nafs* can never find pleasure. This is the sincerity of the ordinary people. Sincerity of the elect is where what happens through them happens without them willing it. Acts of obedience issue from them but they remain separate and unaware of them and do not count them as valuable. That is the sincerity of the elect. (RQ 324)

Ḥīrī: Sincerity is to forget about the creation through constant attention to the Creator. (RQ 324)

Ad-Daqqāq: When one sees shortcomings or flaws in his own sincerity he is on the way toward sincerity. When God wants to make his sincerity pure, He removes his vision of his own sincerity, so that he becomes sincere through God (*mukhlaṣ*) rather than sincere through his own accord (*mukhliṣ*). (RQ 324)

Ḥārith Muḥāsibī: Sincerity means to keep created things out of one's devotional practice towards God, and the *nafs* is the first and foremost created thing. (LT 218)

The Ethics of the Sufis (*akhlāq-i ṣūfiyān*)

Author: The ethics of the sufis are to neither feel offended nor cause offence, and instead to serve and be kind to God's creation in order to win His contentment. Someone who feels offended or causes offence is still somebody, while the sufi is nobody, in that his attributes and characteristics have become annihilated in God.

***

It is reported that one night Bāyazīd was seen coming out of the graveyard. A young man from one of the noble families of Basṭām was playing his lute. When he approached the shaikh, the latter said, "There is no power or strength other than God."

Misunderstanding this, the youth slammed his lute on the shaikh's head, splitting both his skull and the body of the lute! The shaikh returned to the *khānaqāh* and in the morning he sent a servant with the cost of the lute together with a tray of halva to that youth, with instructions to tell him, "Bāyazīd asks for your forgiveness for the fact that your lute broke when it struck his head. Please take this compensation and buy a replacement, and please eat this halva so that the anger and bitterness caused by its breaking will leave your heart."

When the youth heard this, he went to Bāyazīd and fell at his feet, repenting and weeping profusely. Some other youths came and did the same through the grace of the ethics of the shaikh. (TA 171)

I heard that at dawn on the day of festival
Bāyazīd stepped out of the baths
the moment someone poured down ash
from above the exit, unaware he was below.
Ecstatic, he kept rubbing his hands on his turban
and hair,
then rubbed the ash gratefully on his face,
saying: "O nafs, *I am fit for the fire!*
If with one grain of ash my face shrivels up !"

Saʿdī

We will remain steadfast, take the blame,
and remain happy,
for on our path to take offence
is unbelief.

Ḥāfiẓ

Abū ʿAbdallāh Khafīf once fell out with Shaikh Mūsā

ʿImrān Jīruftī. He sent a letter to Jīruftī with the following message: "I have one thousand disciples in Shiraz, and if I ask for one thousand dinars from each of them, I would receive it before the night has passed."

Mūsā ʿImrān sent the following reply: "I have one thousand enemies in Jīruft and if they were to get hold of me they would not hesitate to kill me! Who is the real Sufi then, you or me?" (TSA 539)

Shaikh Abū Ṭālib Khazraj was the master of Abū ʿAbdallāh Khafīf of Shīrāz, who said about him: "While I was serving him he had an ailment in his stomach, with blood spilling out. I placed a basin before him, and when I went away he called out, 'Shīrāzī!' but I could not hear. He called another time, 'Shīrāzī, may God curse you!' and this time I hurried and handed the basin to him."

ʿAlī Daylamī asked Abū ʿAbdallāh Khafīf, "How did you hear that 'May God curse you!' from him?" He answered, "As if he was saying, 'May God bless you!'" (TSA 547)

Junayd said, "Sufis will not step back from the Lord in order to know him for they are seeking nothing less than attainment." (KAM V 196)

When Tirmidhī returned from a journey to Mecca, he discovered that a dog had given birth to puppies in his house, which did not have a locked door. The shaikh did not want to force them out. He came and went eighty times until by its own will the dog took its puppies out. (T 527)

Abū Bakr Warrāq: When you sit down next to a Muslim, do not drive a fly away from yourself, for then you will cause it to buzz away and settle on him instead. (TSA 611)

Anṣārī: One day, Shāh Shujāʿ Kirmānī had sat down in the mosque of some clever men. A poor man stood up and asked for two pieces of bread, but no one gave it to him. Shāh said, "Who will buy the rewards of the fifty pilgrimages I have made to Mecca for two pieces of bread to give to this poor man?"

There was a jurist sitting next to him, who, on hearing this, said, "Shaikh, are you making light of the *sharīʿat*?" He replied, "No, I have never seen either anyone else or myself, and I have not counted the value of anything, so how could I put a price on my own actions." (TSA 237)

Anṣārī was sitting in a shop in Marw with the followers of Ḥāmid when the water-carrier came and poured water for him. For a long while, he kept the water in his cupped hands, so the pourer asked, "Shaikh, why are you not drinking it?" He answered, "A fly is drinking the water, and I am waiting for it to drink its fill, for God's friends do not consume anything at the cost of causing trouble for others." (TSA 625)

It is related that when Bāyazīd was returning from

Mecca, he arrived in Hamadan and bought some seeds, tying the package to his cloak as he made his way back to Basṭām. When he reached there and untied it, he saw a few ants inside, and said, "I have disturbed and displaced them from their home!" He got up and took them back to Hamadan, and placed them back in their home. Unless one values God's command to this extreme, he will not be able to express kind affection towards God's creatures to the same degree. (TA 164)

Ḥamdūn Qaṣṣār: Keep the company of sufis, for vileness is excused by them and goodness is safe there from the danger that they should rate you highly for it and thereby lead you to fall into error. (TA 403)

Junayd: Sufis are a group who stand steadfastly with God, such that they know of nothing but God. (TA 446)

Sahl ibn Ibrāhīm: Once when I was traveling with Ibrahīm Adham I fell ill. He spent all that he had on me. I asked him for something and he sold his donkey and spent the money he received on me. When I had recuperated, I asked him, "Where is the donkey?" He said, "I sold it." I said, "What can I ride on?" He said, "Brother, sit on my shoulders!" He carried me on his shoulders for three days. (RQ 26)

Once when a woman came close to Ḥātim Aṣamm to request something from him, she farted loudly and grew embarrassed. When Ḥātim started to speak, he said, "Speak up!" and acted deaf. That woman then grew happy and spread the news that he cannot hear. The name 'Deaf one' (Aṣamm) became attached to him. (RQ 42)

Etiquette (*adab*)

Author: The sufi's etiquette involves the expression of one's own non-existence before Absolute Existence.

***

Sarī Saqaṭī: Etiquette is the translator of the heart. (TA 338)

ʿAbd Allāh Manāzil: Etiquette is service, but it is not persistence in service which counts, for the correct etiquette in service is dearer than the service itself. (TA 541)

Junayd asked Abū Ḥafṣ Ḥaddād on the latter's arrival in Baghdad, "Have you trained your disciples in the etiquette of kings?" Abū Ḥafṣ replied, "Proper etiquette outwardly corresponds to proper etiquette inwardly." (RQ 481)

Abū ʿAlī Daqqāq: The devotee attains heaven through devotional practice and attains God through etiquette in devotion. (RQ 478)

Jurayrī: For some twenty years I have not even stretched

my legs out in private, for it is most important that one maintain etiquette before God. (RQ 479)

Shiblī: Impudence in addressing God is abandoning etiquette. (RQ 482)

Dhū n-Nūn Miṣrī: The etiquette of the gnostic is higher than all other forms of etiquette, because God is the diciplinary agent of his heart. (RQ 482)

Junayd: When loving-kindness is realized, etiquette prevails. (RQ 484)

Abū ʿAbd Allāh Nibājī: Etiquette is the adornment of the liberated. (TSA 251)

Etiquette and shame have made you
the king of the beautiful people.
Congratulations, for you deserve
such praise a hundredfold.

Ḥāfiẓ

Devotion (*irādat*)

Author: Devotion is God's lasso, pulling the sufi toward Him.

***

Abū ʿAlī ad-Daqqāq: Devotion is a burning in the heart and warmth in the core of the heart, a captivation in the breast, a restlessness in the inner being, and a fire which blazes through hearts. (RQ 311)

Abū ʿUthmān Ḥīrī: Whoever does not have proper devotion from the start will only increase his failure as time passes. (RQ 313)

Kāshānī: Whoever is identified as having devotion yet has something he wishes for in the two worlds other than God, or relaxes for one moment from seeking his wish, does not truly have devotion. (MH 107)

Ibn Khafīf: Devotion draws the heart to seek the object of one's desire, and the essence of that is continual effort and abandonment of rest. (MH 108)

Men and angels feed off love's existence.
Show devotion to gain felicity.

Ḥāfiẓ

Marriage (*izdiwāj*)

Author: Marriage for a person is as necessary as food. Any sufi who refuses to marry of his own accord does harm to his well-being.

***

When a sufi was asked why he did not marry, he replied, "A woman deserves a man, and I have not attained real manhood. How can I marry?"

Another sufi answered in the same vein, saying, "I am more in need of a divorce from my *nafs* than marriage. Once I have divorced my *nafs*, I'll be in a position to take another wife." (MH 255)

When Bishr Ḥāfī was told that people were gossiping about him, he asked what they were saying. He was told, "They are saying that you have refused to marry, even though that is a meritorious act."

"Tell them," replied the master, "that I'm still too occupied with the obligatory to perform the meritorious." (MH 255)

When Ibrāhīm Adham asked a sufi if he was married, the latter replied, "No."

When the master asked if he had any children, the Sufi again replied, "No."

"Very good!" commented the master.

"Why so?", asked the sufi.

"The sufi who is married," replied the master, "is on board a ship. If the sufi has a child, the ship has sunk and he has drowned." (TA 111)

Guide or Master (*ustād* or *pīr*)

Author: The master is the guide of the Path, on the

condition that he has completed the journey and become liberated from self, and will not become a veil between God and people, but instead will call people to God rather than to himself. The guide or master is the one who takes you from yourself and throws you into the lap of God.

***

Ad-Daqqāq: A tree in the wild grows leaves on its own, but the fruit it bears is tasteless. The same holds for a human being. If a person is not cultivated by a guide, such a person will attain nothing. (TA 647)

Ad-Daqqāq: If one intentionally opposes the master, one cannot remain on the Path, one's connection being broken, even though they are in the same house. If, as the disciple of a master, one opposes him in one's heart, one breaks the pledge of discipleship. The only recourse is repentance, although it has been said that it is not possible to repent from faults committed in respect of the master. (TA 653)

Ibrāhīm Shaybānī: If one abandons discipleship of a master, one becomes subject to false claims, leading to disgrace. (TA 719)

The winehouse master in the morning
gave the world-viewing cup to me,

And in that mirror he made
me aware of Your beauty.

Ḥāfiẓ

Choose a master, for without a master
this journey is fraught with blight, fear and danger.

The way you have gone so many times
has made you distraught without a guide.

So don't undertake a way you've not gone
by yourself; don't turn away from the leader!

If you go like a fool without such protection,
the cry of the Devil will lead you astray.

The Devil will throw you off the way into mishap;
those smarter than you have been subject to this.

Mathnawī

Abū l-ʿAbbās: The masters are your mirror; you see them according to the way you are. (TA 642)

Seeking Forgiveness (*istighfār*)

Author: The sufi's existence is a sin for which he must seek forgiveness.

***

Rābiʿa: Seeking forgiveness with the tongue is what liars do. (TA 81)

Dhū n-Nūn: Seeking forgiveness without ceasing to sin is the repentance of liars. (TA 148)

Constancy (*istiqāmat*)

Author: Constancy with God is where nothing which comes along can dint the inward sincerity of the sufi towards God, while constancy with others is where the sufi is never offended by their abuse, answering them with kindness.

***

Jawzjānī: Practice constancy, not miracle-working, for your *nafs* wants miracles, while God wants constancy. (TA 543)

Ad-Daqqāq: Constancy has three aspects: reformation, which disciplines the *nafs*; elevation, which rectifies the heart; and steadfastness, which brings the inner consciousness (*sirr*) closer to God. (RQ 318)

Submission (*islām*)

Author: Submission is that which liberates you from polytheism and self-worship, as you submit to God's will.

***

Muḥammad b. Faḍl Balkhī: Submission frees one from four character traits:

1. not acting on what one knows;
2. acting on what one does not know;
3. not finding out what one does not know; and
4. preventing people from learning. (TA 519)

If this is Submission
which Ḥāfiẓ has,
no tomorrow should come
after today!

Ḥāfiẓ

Allusion and Expression (*ishārat wa ʿibārat*)

Author: Allusion and expression have to do with the world of multiplicity; they do not exist in the realm of Unity.

***

Nūrī: Allusion needs no expression; the inner consciousness must be steeped in sincerity in order to receive allusions from God. (TA 473)

Abū l-ʿAbbās Qaṣṣāb: As long as the distinction between 'I' and 'You' exists, allusion and expression obtain; once they disappear, so do allusion and expression. (TA 643)

God is Greater! (*Allāhu akbar!*)

Author: The meaning of the statement, "God is greater!" is that God is greater than anything which the understanding and the imagination of a created being can encompass.

***

Abū Bakr Wāsiṭī: When a devotee declares, "God is greater!", this means that God is beyond both the attempt to attach oneself to Him and the foreswearing of any action to dissassociate oneself from Him, for neither attachment or disassociation with respect to Him is based on a transitory action but rather something pre-eternally predestined. (TA 746)

When Abū Saʿīd Abī l-Khayr was asked the meaning of 'Allāhu akbar!', he explained, "It means that God's remembrance of His devotee is greater than that of the devotee towards Him."

Ibn Munawwar's commentary: The devotee can remember Him only after God remembers the devotee first. God's remembrance of the devotee is greater, granting the devotee the achievement of remembering God in return. You must bear in mind that God wants to remember Himself, while the devotee is nobody in between. (AT 313)

Absolute Divinity (*ulūhiyyāt*)

Author: In sufi terminology this is a level of Being which encompasses all levels of the Divine Names and Attributes.

***

Rūzbihān: Absolute Divinity is the very essence of God. (SS 632)

Commanding Right and Forbidding Wrong (*amr bi-maʿrūf wa nahī az munkar*)

Author: Wrong is your existence and right is God. Stop existing so that only He exists!

***

Bāyazīd: Try to be in a place where there is no longer any commanding of right and forbidding of wrong, for these two belong to the realm of created beings. In the presence of God's Oneness, there is neither any commanding of right nor forbidding of wrong. (TA 199)

"I am the Truth" (*"anā l-Ḥaqq"*)

Author: Whenever a sufi is annihilated from self and subsists in God, his tongue becomes God's tongue. Another way of putting it is that when a sufi drowns in the Ocean of God's Oneness such that no trace of his self remains, God is the one saying whatever this sufi is saying.

***

Ḥallāj (on being told to say "He is the Truth" instead of "I am the Truth"): I will not do that! All is He. Are you saying that He has become lost that I should have to refer to Him? No, it is I, Ḥusayn, who has become lost. The

All-Encompassing Ocean has neither become lost nor been reduced in any way. (TA 589)

If Manṣūr Ḥallāj says, "I am the Truth",
it means the dust of the whole path has been swept from his eyelashes;

He has dived into the sea of non-existence,
and penetrated as far as "I am the Truth".

Rūmī

Intimacy (*uns*)

Author: The intimacy of the sufi means that he does not settle or feel comfortable with what is other than God.

***

Ruwaym: Intimacy means to retreat from what is other than God. (TA 486)

Mamshād Dīnawarī: The essence of intimacy is to feel appalled by one's *nafs* through remembrance of God. (TSA 260)

Anṭākī: Intimacy means that you become appalled by the world and its people apart from one's own mystic leaders, for intimacy with them is a means of seeking intimacy with God. (TSA 261)

Shiblī: Intimacy means going into seclusion after the ecstasy of *dhikr*. (TSA 260)

Kharrāz: Intimacy is the conversation of spirits with the Beloved in the gatherings of proximity to Him. (TSA 261)

Shiblī: Acquiring intimacy with people is a sure way to become bankrupt spiritually. (TSA 260)

Kharrāz: Intimacy is withdrawing one's heart to the Beloved. (TSA 260)

Junayd: I said something about intimacy to Ḥasan Masūḥī, and then asked him, "What exactly is intimacy?" He replied, "If all of creation under the sky should perish at once, I would not feel horrified." (TSA 260)

Shiblī: Whoever becomes intimate with wealth becomes corrupt; whoever becomes intimate with people becomes dismissed; whoever becomes intimate with deeds becomes preoccupied; whoever becomes intimate with God reaches union with Him. (TSA 623)

The People on the Mystical Path to God (*ahl-i ṭarīq-i Allāh*)

Author: This is what the travelers on the Path to God are called.

***

Rūzbihān: The people on the Path can be classified into three types: the attracted one (*majdhūb*), the drawn one (*ma'khūdh*) and the wayfarer (*sālik*). The attracted one progresses by means of ecstatic states; the wayfarer progresses by means of deeds and stations; the drawn one is annihilated from everything. On reaching God, he even becomes annihilated from annihilation in God. At that time no Path remains for him, for traveling beyond is through the Eternal and the forms of the temporal no longer remain. (SS 406)

Think of an ant as a mighty vanquisher;
think of the thorn as a dagger.
Don't aggravate the tired heart of a gnat,
because from every heart there is a doorway to God.

Shāh Niʿmatullāh Walī

Favoring of Others (*īthār*)

Author: The sufi's favoring of others over himself is manifested by his giving to others that which he needs himself.

***

Muḥammad b. Faḍl: Ascetics favor others over themselves in what they do not need, while the chivalrous favor others over themselves in what they need. (TA 520)

Ad-Daqqāq: Generosity has three stages: generosity itself (*sikhāwat*), munificence (*jūd*), and favoring of others (*īthār*). When one chooses good over oneself, one is being truly generous. When one chooses God over one's heart, one is being munificent. When one chooses God over one's soul, one is practicing *īthār* in the truest sense. (TA 655)

When Ghulām Khalīl launched a policy of hostility against the sufis, he went to the caliph and said, "A group has appeared. They dance and sing and blaspheme and spend every day looking on. They hide in grottos and give speeches. They are heretics. If the Commander of the Faithful decrees for them to be killed, the heretical cult will be eliminated, because this group is the head of all the heretics. If the Commander of the Faithful performs this good deed, I guarantee that it will be of great merit."

Immediately, the caliph ordered the sufis to be brought to him. Those who came were Abū Ḥamza, Raqqām, Shiblī, Nūrī and Junayd. When the caliph ordered them to be executed, the executioner chose Raqqām first. Nūrī stood up and put himself forward in complete sincerity. He sat down in Raqqām's place and said, "Execute me first," smiling in rapture.

"It's not your turn yet," protested the executioner. "The sword canot be rushed."

"My path is based on considering others before myself (*īthār*)," said Nūrī, "and the most precious of things is life itself. I want my brothers to enjoy just a few more moments. So I forfeit my life first. I believe that one moment in the world is worth a thousand years in the hereafter, because this is the domain of service, while that is the domain of nearness, and nearness is based on service."

When the people heard these words from Nūrī, they appealed to the caliph on his behalf. Impressed with the fairness and sincerity on Nūrī's part, the caliph ordered, "Stop the proceedings!" Then he told the judge to deliberate on their case. After interrogating them in a separate chamber, the judge sent a messenger to the caliph, saying, "If they are heretics and blasphemers, I rule that there is no adherent to Divine Unity on earth."

The caliph summoned the sufis and asked what they desired.

"We desire that you forget us," they replied. "You neither honor us by your acceptance, nor do you disgrace us by your rejection, for your rejection is like acceptance to us, and your acceptance, rejection."

The caliph wept profusely and sent them off with the highest of respect. (TA 466)

Faith and Unbelief (*īmān wa kufr*) and Believer and Unbeliever (*mu'min and kāfir*)

Author: Faith is where you devote yourself to God with heart and soul and obey His will.

***

Junayd: The heart is God's special sanctuary. The stalwart is one who lets no outsider in. (TG 646)

Junayd: God respects the believer for that one's faith, a faith which is supported by reason, and reason supported by patience. (MH 382)

Junayd: Unbelief is based on one's being intent on a desire of the body, because the *nafs* cannot be in harmony with the subtlety of surrender to God. Quite the contrary, it is constantly objecting. The objector is a repudiator, and the repudiator is an alien. (KM 251)

When Junayd was asked the difference between the heart of a believer and that of a hypocrite, he replied, "The heart of the believer rotates seventy times an hour, while that of the hypocrite remains in place for seventy years." (TA 449)

The stalwarts of Your Path,
who know the spiritual mystery,
are hidden
from the shortsighted.

The greatest irony is that
whoever comes to know God
becomes a believer
but is called 'unbeliever' by people.

Rūmī

The Idol (*but*)

Author: Whatever lies in your thoughts other than God is your idol.

***

Mamshād Dīnawarī: There are different idols. For some people the idol is one's *nafs*; for some, one's child; for some it is property; for some it is a woman; for some it is one's honor; for some it is the daily prayers (*namāz*), fasting, alms (*zakāt*), and one's inner state.

There are many idols. Every person is attached to one of these idols. No one is free of these idols, unless he is unaware of the state and site of his *nafs* and has no trust in it whatsoever. (TA 611)

The Worst of Times (*badtarīn rūzigār*)

Abū Ḥāzim Makkī: You have fallen on a time when word is accepted over deed and one is satisfied with knowledge over action. So you are stuck among the worst of people in the worst of times. (TA 67)

Staring at Others (*bisyār nigarīstan bi dīgarān*)

Author: From the sufi point of view, staring at the master's face and becoming dazzled is considered bad conduct.

***

When someone visited Dā'ūd Ṭā'ī and kept staring at him, the master said, "Don't you know that staring too much is as objectionable as babbling nonsense?" (RQ 36)

Devoteeship (*bandagī* or *'ubūdiyat*)

Author: Devoteeship is shedding the shackles of your self, as you become ensnared in God's lasso.

***

Junayd: Devoteeship means liberation from enslavement to others. (TA 449)

Abū l-ʿAbbās Qaṣṣāb: Others seek to be free from God, while I seek to be enslaved to Him in devoteeship, for God's slave stays away from danger, while one who seeks to be free from Him is headed toward destruction. (TA 642)

Abū l-Ḥasan Kharaqānī: The sign of devoteeship is that the 'I' in the devotee is a manifestation of God, so that there is no manifestation of devoteeship at all. (TA 711)

Junayd: The characteristics of devoteeship are utter abasement, helplessness, abjectness and being still, while that of Lordship is all grandeur and omnipotence. (TA 447)

Abū ʿAlī Jawzjānī: Contentment is the chamber of devoteeship and patience the door to it, while commitment (*tafwīḍ*) is its house. A voice comes from behind the door; relief is within the chamber; and ease is in the house. (RQ 307)

Sahl b. ʿAbd Allāh Tustarī: The first station of devoteeship is the shedding of free will, as one becomes weary of one's own will and power. (TA 315)

Yūsuf b. Ḥusayn: The ultimate devoteeship is being God's devotee in everything. (TA 389)

Nūrī: Devoteeship is the witnessing of Lordship. (TA 473)

Abū Bakr Wāsiṭī: The ordinary are concerned with the attributes of devoteeship, while the elect are dignified with those of Lordship, so that they may witness. The ordinary do not have the strength to bear these attributes, because of the weakness of their inner consciousness and their distance from what issues from God. (TA 743)

Ad-Daqqāq: Devoteeship is more complete than devotional practice (*ʿibādat*). First, there is devotional practice, then devoteeship, and finally devout adoration (*ʿubūdat*). Devotional practice belongs to the ordinary believer, devoteeship to the elect, and devout adoration to the elect of the elect. (RQ 303)

Ad-Daqqāq: Devotional practice belongs to those at the level of striving; devoteeship to those at the level of enduring; and devout adoration to those at the level of witnessing. Whoever does not withhold his self from God is at the level of devotional practice. Whoever does not withhold his heart from God is at the level of devoteeship. Whoever does not withhold his spirit from God is at the level of devout adoration. (RQ 303)

Jurayrī: There are many devotees of God's bounty but few devotees of the Bountiful One Himself. (RQ 304)

It has been said that devoteeship means dismissing one's

own achievement and efforts, and acknowledging that whatever comes to one is entirely through the grace, bounty and favor of God. (RQ 303)

Heaven and Hell (*bihisht wa dūzakh*)

Author: The sufi's heaven is closeness to God, and the sufi's hell is distance from Him. Hell is in the world of the ego; when you are liberated from it, everywhere is heaven.

***

Junayd (on emerging from the congregational mosque after prayers, seeing a large crowd and turning to his disciples): These all have the potential for heaven, but one who sits with God is of a different order. (TA 428)

Imām Jaʿfar Ṣādiq: God has a heaven in the world and a hell. The heaven is soundness, and the hell affliction. Soundness is consigning your work to God, and affliction is handing over God's work to your *nafs*. (TA 18)

The garden of heaven, the shade of Ṭūbā
and castles with houris:

For me these cannot match the dust
of the lane of the Beloved.

Ḥāfiẓ

Shiblī (when asked why he was carrying a stick with both ends aflame): I am going to burn up hell with one end and heaven with the other so that people will pay attention to God alone. (TA 617)

Abū l-Ḥasan Kharaqānī: I do not say that heaven and hell do not exist. I only say that they have no place with me, for both are created, and wherever I am, what is created has no place. (TA 677)

Abū Saʿīd b. Abī l-Khayr: Wherever 'you' exist is hell completely, and wherever 'you' are not, is heaven completely. (AT 221)

Ad-Daqqāq: I have nothing to do with either heaven or hell. For me there is only joy with subsistence in God. (KAM VIII 520)

Abū ʿAlī Siyāh: The one who worships God for the sake of reward is the devotee of reward, not of God. (KAM IX 155)

I have a tongue
different from this tongue;

I have a place
different from heaven and hell.

Those with liberated hearts
have a different life;
and that pure jewel of theirs
is from a different mine.

Rūmī

Into my grip comes the pain and
agony from Your tresses;
I am pining for the state
of those who dwell in heaven.

You say that I will be taken
to heaven,
but heaven is not big enough
for my heart.

Rūmī

They say that paradise
will consist of these things:
fine wine and lovely houris
will be found there.

I already have
the wine and Beloved in hand,
because the end of things
will be thus anyway.

Rūmī

My father sold paradise
for just two grains of wheat;
I won't be in the wrong
if I sell it for a grain of barley.

Ḥāfiẓ

Practice of Poverty (*parsa*)

Author: Poverty was the sufis' going out in the streets with the aim of breaking themselves. They would repeat a word or a phrase or a poem, and to passersby they would offer a green leaf or something like rosewater or mint. In return the recipients might toss something into the sufis' bowls (*kashkul*s). The sufis would then take whatever they had in their bowls to their place of gathering and share it with one another. This practice of poverty was a custom especially of the Khāksārī dervishes.

Detachment from the World (*tajrīd*)

Author: Detachment from the world is detaching yourself from whatever is other than God.

***

When one sits humbly on the earth,
leaf and blossom sprout forth.
When the seed sinks into the earth,
a shoot sprouts up therefrom.

You must be detached from the world
to follow the Path to the end.
When the chrysalis bursts,
the butterfly comes forth.

ʿAṭṭār

Yūsuf b. Ḥusayn: When one has plunged into the sea of detachment from the world, one becomes daily ever more thirsty, and one's thirst is never quenched, for one's thirst is for Reality, and that can be slaked only by God. (TA 388)

Junayd: Detachment from the world occurs when one's outward aspect is detached from effects and one's inward from objections. (TA 447)

Fear (*tars*)

Author: Fear besets the ego. To the extent that the sufi has no ego, he has no fear.

***

Abū l-Qāsim Ḥakīm: Fear is of two kinds: fright and dread. The frightened turn tail and run away from God, while those in dread run to Him for refuge. (RQ 191)

Since our fear was once
of becoming afflicted,
now what should we fear
while in the throes of affliction?

Rūmī

Sufism (*taṣawwuf*), the Sufi (*ṣūfī*), the Sufiologist (*mutaṣawwif*), the Dervish (*darwīsh*) and Dervishness (*darwīshī*)

Author: The sufi is one who is liberated from self and has joined with God.

The word *ṣūfī*, is the direct equivalent of the Persian word *darwīsh*. The school of chivalry and spiritual poverty originated in Greater Khurasan, from where it passed to Arabia. Coming from those colder climes, the dervishes who came from Iran wore fleece-coats, as they still do. When the Arabs saw them in this attire of wool, which in Arabic is *ṣūf*, they named the Iranian dervishes after their dress. There is no other derivation of the word 'sufi' in the Arabic language.

***

Junayd: Sufism is God making you die from yourself and bringing you to life in Him. (TA 441)

Junayd: The sufi is a plot of ground into which all the waste has been thrown and from which all good things issue forth. And he is like the cloud whose shadow covers everything and the rain which pours on everything. (TA 440)

Abū ʿAbd Allāh Turūghbudī: The sufi is preoccupied with God, while the ascetic is preoccupied with the *nafs*. (TA 557)

Abū l-Ḥasan Kharaqānī: The dervish is one who possesses neither the world nor the hereafter, desiring neither, for they are too petty for the heart to be connected with. (TA 695)

Bāyazīd: Sufism is where in a corner of one's heart one steps into the treasure known as 'disgrace for the hereafter' and discovers the gem known as 'loving-kindness'. Whoever finds this gem is a dervish. (TA 199)

Ḥuṣrī: The sufi is one who, having become released from the flaws of temporality, does not lapse back into them. When such a one directs his gaze towards God, he does not cease to look upon Him and the transitory has no effect on him. (TA 761)

Ḥusrī: The sufi is one who has no being when his self becomes non-existent and who does not become non-existent after gaining True Being. (TA 761)

Ḥuṣrī: The sufi is one whose ecstasy (*wajd*) is his being (*wujūd*) and whose attributes are his veil; or, as the Tradition states, "One who knows oneself knows one's Lord." (TA 761)

Ḥuṣrī: Sufism is the purification of the heart from all qualities of opposition. (TA 761)

ʿAlī Rūdbārī: Sufism is the quintessence of nearness, purged of the turbidity of distance. (TA 756)

ʿAlī Rūdbārī: Sufism is the purity of nearness to God that occurs after the impurity of being far from Him, and also clinging to the door of the Friend, making the threshold your pillow, however much you are driven away. (TA 756)

ʿAlī Rūdbārī: Sufism is the divine gift to the liberated. (TA 756)

Junayd: The sufis are so committed to God that only God

knows them. (TA 446)

Abū Bakr Kattānī: Sufis are outwardly slaves and inwardly free. (TSS 375)

Kattānī: The sufi is one who considers his own act of obedience to be a sin for which he must seek forgiveness. (TA 568)

Shiblī: One is not a sufi until one sees the whole of creation as one's family. (TA 631)

Shiblī: The sufis are children gathered around God. (RQ 472)

Muḍaffar Kirmānshāhī: The dervish is one who is beyond appealing to God to fulfill his needs. (RQ 461)

Nūrī: The sufis are that group whose souls have become liberated from the impurity of human nature, purified of the pestilence of the *nafs*, and freed from ego-desire, so that they have become tranquil in God's foremost rank and highest degree, having bolted from what is other than God, being neither possessors nor the possessions of anyone. (TA 473)

Abū l-Ḥasan Būshangī: Sufism is today a name, where that which is named is not apparent, and was previously a reality which had no name. (TA 522)

Kharaqānī: The sufi is the one whose heart is not

affected by conceptions. He speaks without utterance, sees without vision, hears without audition, and eats without tasting. He experiences neither motion nor rest, neither joy nor sorrow.

Kharaqānī also said: God says, "I have created all the creation, but I have not created the sufi." This means that the sufi, being nothing, is not created. In other words, the sufi is of the domain of the Command ["Be!"], not that of the creation. (TA 701)

Jaʿfar Khuldī: Sufism is a condition in which the essence of Lordship appears in a sufi, while the essence of devoteeship disappears. (TA 753)

Abū Bakr b. Yazdānyār: The sufis of Khorasan have deeds but no words, while the sufis of Baghdad are the opposite. Then again the sufis of Basra have both, while the sufis of Egypt have neither. (TA 335)

Abū ʿUthmān Maghribī: The sufi is one who owns things by authority, but nothing owns him by force of imposition. (TSS 480)

Abū l-Ḥusayn Nūrī: The sufi neither possesses nor is possessed by anything. (TA 473)

Nūrī: Sufism is neither knowledge nor custom. Rather, it is a matter of temperament. This means that if Sufism were custom, it would be acquired by personal effort, and if it were knowledge, it would be obtained by instruction. Being a case of temperament, it is described by the expression: “Be graced with God’s temperament.” As such, one ends up with God’s temperament, not with either custom or knowledge. (TA 473)

Nūrī: Sufism is freedom; it is chivalry (*jawānmardī*); it is the abandonment of pretension; and it is generosity. (TA 473)

Nūrī: Sufism is hostility to the world and friendship with God. (TA 473)

Ruwaym: Sufism is based on three qualities:

1. committing oneself to spiritual poverty;
2. realizing selflessness and favoring others (*īthār*); and
3. abandoning objection and self-will. (TA 485)

Ruwaym: Sufism means being steadfast in performing virtuous deeds. (TA 485)

Ibn Jalāʾ: The sufi is a pauper who is detached from secondary causes. (TA 498)

Murtaʿish: Sufism means having a good temperament. (TA 517)

Murtaʿish: Sufism is a state which makes the possessor thereof absent from speech, carrying him to God, the Bestower of Kindness. Then it takes him from there, so that God alone remains and he does not exist. (TA 517)

Murtaʿish: Sufism is the most serious of religions, so don't mix with it any levity! (TA 517)

Abū Turāb Nakhshabī: Nothing makes the sufi turbid, and all that is turbid becomes purified by such a one. (RQ 473)

Muḥammad b. Faḍl: The sufi is one who is purified of all ills and not concerned with any bounties. (TA 519)

Abū l-Ḥasan Būshanjī: Sufism means desisting from hope and persisting in action. (TA 522)

Kattānī: Sufism is all temperament. The more virtuous one's temperament is, the greater one's Sufism. (TA 568)

Kattānī: Sufism is purity and witnessing. (TA 568)

Ibn Khafīf: The sufi is one who wears wool (*ṣūf*) in purity, rejects desire as bitter to the taste, and tosses the world behind his back. (TA 577)

Ibn Khafīf: Sufism is patience in the face of the onflow of determined events, acceptance of what comes from God, and covering the distances of deserts and mountains. (TA 577)

Mamshād Dīnawarī: Sufism is purity of inner being, acting in accordance with God's pleasure, and associating with others without volition. (TA 612)

Dīnawarī: Sufism means to be generous while remaining anonymous so that people do not find out that the sufi is the agent, and it means avoiding what does not serve one's purpose on the Path. (TA 612)

Kharaqānī: The sufi is a day which requires no sunlight and a moonless, starless night which requires neither moon nor stars. (TA 700)

Abū l-Ḥasan Sīrwānī: The sufi is involved with infusions (*wāridāt*) in the heart, not with litanies (*awrād*) on the tongue. (RQ 474)

Hujwīrī: The sufi is of three types:

1. The sufi proper, who is annihilated from self and subsistent in God, liberated from the constriction of the dictates of material nature and connected to the reality of truths.
2. The potential sufi, who seeks the aforementioned level by spiritual striving, constantly seeking to perform the devotions of the realized Sufis correctly.
3. The would-be sufi, who imitates the sufis for the sake of achievement, status, and pleasure in the world.

This last one has no clue about the previous types, and is so different from them that it is said, "The would-be sufi is as worthless as a fly in the view of the real sufi." (KM 40)

Junayd: Sufism is an attribute in which the devotee dwells. When asked whether this is a Divine or a human attribute, he added: Its reality is Divine, while its form of expression is human.

Hujwīrī's commentary: This means that its reality is the consequence of the devotee's attributes being annihilated in the subsistence of the Attributes of God. Thus it is a Divine Attribute. Its expression is the result of the devotee's spiritual striving becoming continuous, and this is the attribute of the devotee. (KM 41)

Nūrī: Sufism means abandonment of all pleasures of the *nafs*, and this is of two kinds:

1. In form, where one's very abandonment of pleasure is a pleasure in itself.
2. In essence, where pleasure abandons the devotee, resulting in the end of pleasure. This is linked to the essence of witnessing.

Thus, the abandonment of pleasure is the act of the devotee, whereas the bringing to an end of pleasure is the act of God. (KM 42)

Nūrī: The sufis are those who have become free from the impurity of their human nature, free from the affliction of the *nafs*, and liberated from ego-desire, so that they have found tranquillity in the front rank and supreme degree with God. (KM 42)

Ibn Jalāʾ: Sufism is an essence which has no form.

Whatever involves form belongs to human beings in the form of devotions, whereas the essence is particular to God. Since Sufism means turning away from human beings, it inevitably has no form. (KM 43)

Abū ʿAmr Dimashqī: Sufism means that you look at the realm of existence as being imperfect, and this shows the subsistence of human attributes. Therefore, you raise your eyes from the realm of existence, and this leads to annihilation of human attributes. (KM 43)

Ḥuṣrī: Sufism is the purification of the innermost level of the heart from the pollution of discord.

Hujwīrī's commentary: This means guarding the innermost level of the heart from opposing God. This is because love means agreement and agreement is the opposite of opposition. (KM 43)

Imam Muḥammad Bāqir: Sufism is goodness of disposition. Whoever has a better disposition is a better sufi.

Hujwīrī's commentary: Goodness of disposition is of two kinds: the first in relation to God and the second in relation to other people. Goodness of disposition in relation to God means contentment with His decree, while goodness of disposition in relation to people means enduring the burden of their company for the sake of God. Both of these kinds are of concern only to the seeker, for God is free from concern about the contentment or displeasure of the seeker. (KM 44)

Murtaʿish: The sufi is one whose thoughts are in accord with his footsteps.

Hujwīrī's commentary: This means he is completely present and his heart is in the place where his body is and his body is where his heart is; his words are where his footsteps are, and his footsteps are where his words are. This is a sign of presence without any absence. In disagreement, some say that the sufi is absent from himself and present with God. This is not so, for he is both present with God and with himself, and this is an expression of absolute union (*jamʿ al-jamʿ*), seeing as there can be no absence from self while there is vision of oneself. When vision of oneself goes, presence without any absence comes. (KM 44)

ʿAlī ibn Bundār Nīshāpūrī: Sufism is where the sufi does not see his own exterior or interior, and instead sees everything as God. (KM 46)

Abū Ḥafṣ Ḥaddād Nīshāpūrī: Sufism is all manners, for every moment, station and state has its own particular manners. Whoever observes the appropriate manners for each circumstance will reach the level of great men, and whoever does not will end up far from thought of proximity to God and will be denied belief in God's acceptance of him. (KM 47)

Murtaʿish: Sufism means good character, and this is of three types: the first is in relation to God and means obeying God's commands without pretension; the second is in relation to people and means respecting superiors, being kind to inferiors, and being fair to one's equals, while not seeking justice or reward from any of them; the third is in relation to oneself and means not acting on lust or Satan. Whoever makes himself fulfill all three types can be counted as one of those who truly have good character. (KM 47)

Murtaʿish: This school of Sufism is all seriousness, so do not mix joking with it.

Hujwīrī's commentary: Do not adhere to the ways of the superficial ones, and flee from those who emulate them! (KM 48)

Abū ʿAlī Qarmīsinī: Sufism is pleasing ethics. (KM 48)

Nūrī: Sufism is freedom, chivalry, generosity, and the abandonment of hardships.

Hujwīrī's commentary: Freedom is what liberates a slave from the shackles of lust, and true chivalry is what separates him from viewing his own chivalry. Abandonment of hardships means not striving after benefit or reward, and generosity means leaving the world to worldly people. (KM 48)

Nūrī: Sufism is cutting off all pleasure from the *nafs*. (TSS 166)

Shiblī: Sufism is harmony and mutual affection. (TSS 340)

Murtaʿish: Sufism means obscurity, covering up, and concealment. (TSS 352)

Abū l-Ḥasan Ḥuṣrī hailed from Basra but resided in Baghdad, where he was originally a disciple of Shiblī. He regularly held sessions of spiritual audition (*samāʿ*) with his disicples. Word went to the caliphal court that he and his disciples were a particularly disruptive group, singing and dancing, going constantly into ecstasy and rapture, while performing *samāʿ*.

Once the caliph was out riding in the countryside when Ḥuṣrī and his disciples happened along. A courtier pointed him out to the caliph, saying, "There is the man who claps his hands and pounds his feet!"

The caliph reined in and hailed the master, asking, "What is your religious affiliation?"

"I followed the school of Abū Ḥanīfa at first," he replied. "Then I went to that of Shāfiʿī. Now I am involved in something which is beyond any school of jurisprudence."

On being asked what that school was, Ḥuṣrī said simply, "That of the sufi."

When the caliph asked what a sufi was, he replied, "One who cannot attain tranquillity or peace in the two worlds without God."

The caliph asked him to explain further. So he said, "Such a one consigns his affairs to his God, whereby in effect he manages his own destiny."

The caliph pressed him to tell more. So he explained, "Without God one can only go astray. When the sufis find God, they look at nothing else."

The caliph ordered that the sufis be left alone, "For they are a great people, whose work God has in hand." (TA 759)

Maghribī: Sufism means the severance of attachments, the rejection of created beings, and integration with realities." (TA 785)

Maʿrūf Karkhī: Sufism means receiving truths, speaking subtly, and having no faith in anything in the hands of created beings. (TA 327)

Qushayrī: If one tries to adopt sufi practices, he is a sufi aspirant (*mutaṣawwif*). And the word 'sufi' cannot be understood in terms of some other words. There are no other derivations of this word in the Arabic language. The most obvious understanding is that it is a descriptive title (*laqab*), as if someone were to say "He is of wool", making '*taṣawwuf*' mean 'the wearing of wool'. That is one possibility but this group is not distinguished just by the wearing of wool!

If one claims that the word derives from *ṣuffa*, the 'raised area' of the Prophet's mosque, this has to be erroneous, because it comes from a different Arabic root.

If one claims that it stems from *ṣafāʾ* ('purity'), this would be too remote a derivation both etymologically and semantically.

Then again, if one chooses to relate it to *ṣaff-i awwal*, the 'front row' of those performing the congregational prayer, connoting closeness to God, the semantics would be correct, but the etymology would be wrong.

The fact of the matter is that this group is too venerable to be relegated to a mere etymological derivation. (RQ 468)

A dervish wearing sackcloth and a coarse gunny hat came to Abū ʿAlī Ad-Daqqāq. One of the sufis was curious to know how much the sackcloth had cost. "I bought it with the world," replied the dervish. "Then the hereafter was offered to me for it in return, but I refused to sell it." (RQ 454)

Abū Saʿīd b. Abī l-Khayr: Sufism is the heart's standing with God without intermediary. (KM 207)

Abū Saʿīd: I paid a visit to Abū Bakr Jawzafī and asked him to transmit a Prophetic Tradition to me. So he recounted the one concerning God having two armies, one in heaven decked out in green, and one on earth, being the troops of Khorasan. At the present time these troops are the sufis, who will take over the entire earth. (AT 267)

Abū Saʿīd: A hundred masters have spoken of Sufism. The first has said the same as the last. The expressions have varied, but the meaning has been the same, namely, that Sufism is the renunciation of affectation, and there is no greater affectation for you than your very you-ness. (AT 216)

One day Abū Saʿīd was riding with a group of disciples when they arrived at the door of a mill. They decided to stop to linger for a while. "Do you know what this mill is saying?", asked the master. "It says, 'Sufism is what I have. I take the coarse and return it fine, while rotating round myself. I travel within myself, to drive away what should not be produced by me.'" The disciples then all enjoyed a rapturous state. (AT 287)

Abū Saʿīd: Sufism means giving up what you have in your head, giving away what you have in your hand, and not being bothered by whatever comes your way. (AT 297)

Abū Saʿīd: Sufism is two things: looking in one direction and seeing all as one and the same. (AT 297)

In the course of a meeting Abū Saʿīd once said, "This Sufism is honor in lowliness, wealth in poverty, mastery in servitude, repleteness in hunger, being clothed in nakedness, freedom in slavery, life in death, sweetness in bitterness. Whoever enters this Path and does not travel with these qualities will every day go more astray. (AT 302)

He said, "No dervish exists in the world,
And, if there is one, that dervish does not exist.
He exists from the viewpoint of subsisting
in God's essence,
But his qualities have become effaced in His qualities.

Mathnawī

Abū Saʿīd: The sufis are not themselves. If they were, they would not be sufis. Their name is their attribute.

Whoever seeks the way to God must pass by way of the sufis who are the gate to God. (AT 307)

Abū Saʿīd (upon being asked why God may be seen but not the sufi): Because God exists, and the existent may be seen, whereas the sufi does not exist, and one cannot see the non-existent. (AT 313)

Kharaqānī: The sufi is a dead body, a living heart, and a burnt-up soul. (TSA 431)

Dhū n-Nūn: The sufi is one who tirelessly seeks and is never upset over something taken from him. (LT 25)

Dhū n-Nūn: The sufis have chosen God over everything. Thus, God has chosen them over everything. (LT 25)

Dhū n-Nūn: The sufi is one who, when he gives an explanation his speech represents the realities of his state, meaning that he would not say anything that had not been realized in his own being. When he is silent, his actions are consistent with his state. When he speaks, it is in a condition of severance of attachments. This means that his speech is entirely on a sound foundation. His actions are all in a state of complete detachment. When he speaks, his words are all Divine. When he is silent, his actions are entirely selfless. (TA 150)

Nūrī: The most aware people are the sufis, for the rest head towards His bounty, but the sufis have advanced to God Himself, seeking association with Him. The rest are fully content with what He has given to them, while the sufis have never been content with any substitute for Him. They have not sought or gained this for themselves, for whenever they have seen something, their eyes have been raised to Him. All attachments have fallen from them, and they have dissolved completely in Him.

The rest of mankind have all advanced to the Attributes, through which they have become content with the attributes, as distinguished from the Possessor of the Attributes. The sufis have advanced to the Essence, seeing nothing but Him. For them the whole world is rejected, and the more they know, the more they reject it. The fact is that if one does not know oneself, one is simply helpless and not in a position to reject. Only one who knows can reject. (TSA 72)

Anṣārī: Ordinary people say, "One," but approach a thousand different doors. The sufis say, "One," and flee from every sign of themselves. (TSA 94)

Abū l-Hasan Sīrwanī: Sufism means focusing one's aspiration (*himmat*) on the One and living, while among others, only with the One. (TSA 567)

Abū ʿAlī Ad-Daqqāq: The sufi is neither in the ranks of the world nor even classed as a human being. He belongs to a clan called 'non-being'. (TSA 531)

Abū Muḥammad Rāsibī: A sufi is not a sufi until not a scrap of land belongs to him nor does the sky cause him to cast a shadow nor is he accepted by others. He is focused on God alone. (TSS 513)

Abū Sulaymān Dārānī: Sufism is seeing everything that happens to one as coming from God alone. The sufi is constantly with God in such a way that he knows only God. (TA 281)

Ruwaym: The sufi has no state or station, for the sufi has transcended states and stations. (TSA 264)

Ruwaym: Sufism is the abandonment of having preferences between two things. (TSA 264)

ʿAlī b. Sahl Iṣfahāni: In my view it is not right to call the sufis, 'dervishes' [meaning 'the poor'], for they are the richest of all people. (TSA 283)

Abū Yaʿqūb Mazābilī: Sufism is a state in which the characteristics of human nature are obliterated. (TSA 337)

Abū Bakr b. Abī Saʿdān: The sufi is beyond descriptions and formalities. (TSA 465)

Ḥuṣrī: The sufi's ecstasy (*wajd*) is the sufi's finding of True Being (*wujūd*), and the sufi's attributes are the sufi's veil. (TSA 530)

ʿAbd Allāh Kharrāz (quoted by Abū ʿAbd Allāh Muqrī): Among the inspirations of the friends of God (*awliyāʾ*) is the sufi saying: "You may authenticate the sincere ones by what is said of them and of their masters." (TSS 512)

Abū Ḥafṣ Ḥaddād: Sufism is all etiquette. (TA 399)

Shiblī (on being asked why the sufis were named so): Because a remnant of their *nafs* remains. If that were not the case, there would be nothing to name. (RQ 473)

Bāyazīd: God purges the sufis of their own attributes. Then He bestows purity (*ṣafā'*) on them and calls them '*ṣūfī*'. (T 331)

Junayd: Sufism is sitting for an hour with God without self-will.

Anṣārī's commentary: What does 'without self-will' mean? Finding without seeking and seeing without looking, for the viewer is disabled when conscious of viewing. (TSA 201)

Bayazīd: Sufism is an Attribute of God which the devotee hides. (NKAT 85)

Junayd: Sufism is God's slaying the sufi from himself and bringing him to life in Him. (TA 441)

Dhū n-Nūn (on being asked whether Sufism is a derivation or a title): In essence it is derived from *ṣafawiyat*, meaning 'quintessence', the 'utmost of purity'. God hid this *ṣafā'* or 'purity' with *taṣawwuf* ('Sufism'), meaning that in practice whatever causes hypocrisy is to be covered by purity. (KD 113)

Shiblī: Sufism is being how you are as you were when you did not exist.

He also said: Sufism means restraint of the senses and observance of breaths.

And he also said: Sufism means chastity with respect to viewing the realm of existence.

And: Sufism means sitting in the presence of God with no sense of sorrow. (TA 631)

Shiblī: Sufism means not being fulfilled by anything other than God. (RQ 460)

Shiblī: Sufism means bringing peace to hearts by fanning them with purity (*ṣafā*) and elevating minds by enveloping them with fidelity (*wafā*), becoming graced with the attribute of generosity and cheerful with every encounter. (TB XIV 391)

Shiblī: Sufism is polytheism in the sense that the heart is protected from seeing what is other than God, yet there is nothing other than God.

Hujwīrī's commentary: In affirming adherence to Divine Unity (*tawḥīd*), the seeing of what is other than God is polytheism. Since in the heart what is other than God has no validity, keeping the heart from being conscious of what is other than God is pointless. (KM 43)

Shiblī: The sufi is one who sees nothing but God in the two worlds. Insofar as the devotee is other than God, when he does not see what is other than God he does not see himself. He becomes completely liberated from self, neither denying nor affirming himself. (KM 44)

Dīnawarī: The most exalted forms of knowledge in Sufism are that of the Names and Attributes, and the distinction between purification of outward actions and soundness of inward states. (TSS 516)

Rūzbihān: Sufism is Divine Unity (*tawḥīd*) and the sufi is the adherent to Divine Unity. The condition for being a sufi is to be effaced from self and all existence, effaced under the assaults of Unity. One reaches the point of affirming Universal nature under the condition of negating created nature. Thereupon one becomes annihilated from the effacement, affirmation and formation of oneself in adherence to Divine Unity and gnosis. In seeking the witnessing of the Eternal, one emerges from the custom of transitoriness. Then only God remains as He was in pre-eternity prior to His effacement and affirmation, for these states are the properties of transitoriness, and transitoriness is not evident in the Eternal. (SS 416)

Exegesis or Interpretation (*tafsīr*)

Author: The sufis say that if you want to interpret something, then start with yourself and know yourself.

***

Kharaqānī: I have seen people who occupy themselves

with interpreting the Koran. The chivalrous (*jawānmardān*) are occupied with interpreting themselves. (TA 709)

Reflection (*tafakkur* or *fikr*)

Author: The sufi reflects on God's bounties, signs and attributes, which lead one from falsity to the Truth, so that one sees the Absolute Being through the existential manifestations.

***

Junayd: Reflection has several aspects. There is reflection on Divine signs, and the sign of this is that it produces gnosis (*maʿrifa*). There is reflection on God's blessings and bounties, and from this springs loving-kindness. There is reflection on God's promise and threat, from which comes awe. There is reflection on the attributes of the *nafs* and on God's beneficence towards it, whence springs shame before God.

If one were to ask why reflection on God's promise should engender awe, I say that if one depends on God's munificence, then one flees from God and lapses into transgression. (TA 447)

Abū Saʿīd (on being asked to interpret the saying: "One hour's reflection is better than a year's devotional practice."): One hour's concentration on one's non-existence is better than a whole year of devotional practice while conscious of one's existence. (AT 318)

Dhū n-Nūn: Reflection on God's Essence is ignorance, pointing to God is polytheism, and the reality of gnosis is bewilderment. (TSA 109)

Reflection should be such
that it opens a way;
the Way should be such
that a king comes along it.

The king is the one
who is king in Himself,
not a king in terms
of treasures and armies.

Mathnawī

Reflection means to go from falsity to the Truth,
to view within the particular the Absolute Universal.
The condition for worthy reflection is detachment,
after which comes a flash of the lightning of
confirmation.

Shabistarī

Piety (*taqwā*)

Author: Piety means restraining yourself from whatever displeases God.

***

Aḥmad Masrūq: Piety is not peering at the pleasures of the world out of the corner of your eye nor coveting them in your heart. (TA 555)

Ibn Khafīf: Piety means being distant from whatever distances you from God. (TA 578)

Muḥammad b. ʿAlī Tirmidhī: If no one can claim anything from you at the Resurrection, this is piety; if you cannot claim anything from anyone else, this is chivalry. (TA 532)

Qushayrī: The basis of piety is to avoid polytheism, then to avoid transgressions and evils, then to avoid suppositions, then to abandon all that is superfluous. (RQ 161)

Abū Bakr Wāsiṭī: True piety is to become purified of your very piety, that is, of being conscious of it. (RQ 162)

This piety of mine is enough
to keep me from flouncing about

and flirting from the pulpit,
like the preachers of the town.

Ḥāfiẓ

Magnification [of God's Name] (*takbīr*)

Author: The sufi's magnification of God is to renounce everything other than God.

***

Kharaqānī: I made eighty magnifications: one before renouncing the world, the second in renouncing the creation, the third in renouncing the *nafs*, the fourth in renouncing the hereafter, the fifth preceding pious obedience. These I can reveal to others, but the rest I cannot. (TA 688)

The moment that I did
ablution at the wellspring of love
I gave the four magnifications of the funeral prayer
in renouncing everything that is.

Ḥāfiẓ

Fluctuation (*talwīn*), Stability (*tamkīn*), Extinction (*iṣṭilām*) and Effacement (*maḥw*)

Author: Fluctuation is the attribute of beginners, and stability that of those who have completed the Path. Extinction represents the emergence from selfhood and sensations, leading ultimately to effacement.

***

Qushayrī: Fluctuation is the attribute of those who enjoy states, and stability that of those who share realities. As long as the devotee is traveling the Path, he is in fluctuation, going constantly from state to state and from attribute to attribute. Once he leaves this station and arrives at a higher one, he has attained stability.

One in fluctuation is constantly gaining more, while one in stability has reached the final point, attaining Union, the sign of which is that one has become wholly negated from one's whole self.

The masters have said that the journey of the seekers ends where they have conquered their *nafs* and thereupon attained Union. The reason for this is the disappearance of the dictates of human nature. Once the domination of Reality overcomes one, when one remains constantly in this state, one is in stability.

The masters also say that as long as the devotee continues to travel the stations, he can expect to experience increase and decrease in states in his attributes. When he reaches the Divine, with the disappearance of the dictates of his human nature, God brings him to stability.

Know that he does not gain knowledge of the self. He becomes stable in his state in accordance with his situation. God sends gifts for him with any given breath, the measure of which is limitless. Thus, he moves steadily into one condition ever more sublime than the other. So he proceeds from the preceding stations just to the point where there is none higher, because there can be no superfluity in God's measures in any given context.

Now for the one who has become extinguished from his self and has transcended the senses, given that human nature necessarily has its limits: when he has become annihilated from everything—from *nafs* and sensation, indeed, all created things—this absence will be permanent for him, and he is utterly effaced. Here neither stability nor fluctuation, neither honor nor religious obligation, remains unless God brings him back to consciousness of what is happening to him without his intention. Others think that such a one is in control in the world, whereas, in fact, he is under the control of Reality. (RQ 131)

Would-be Ecstasy (*tawājud*), Ecstasy (*wajd*) and True Being (*wujūd*)

Author: Would-be ecstasy means consciously trying to be in ecstasy. Ecstasy is a powerful infusion (*wārid*) which brings complete immersion and causes yearning. The ecstatic has no resistance in the face of this. It stimulates emotion in one, be it joy or sorrow. Ecstasy carries one to True Being, which obliterates one.

***

ʿAmr b. ʿUthmān Makkī: There is no way of explaining ecstasy, for it is God's mystery in the believers. (RQ 59)

Qushayrī: Would-be ecstasy is the conscious effort on the part of the seeker to bring on ecstasy, which is never completely realized by such a one in that one can properly be considered an ecstatic only when one's ecstasy is complete.

Ecstasy itself must come into your heart without effort on your part. For this reason masters have said that ecstasy must be 'found'. Found experiences are infusions. The more committed one is, the more of God's subtleties one receives.

I heard the master Abū ʿAlī Daqqaq say, "Would-be ecstasy may bring the devotee to proper ecstasy, which in turn will lead him to complete immersion. Ultimately True Being will cause one to be obliterated. Would-be ecstasy belongs to beginners, while True Being belongs to those who have completed the Path, with ecstasy in the middle, between the beginning and the end. (RQ 98)

Humility (*tawāḍuʿ*)

Author: Humility is considering yourself nobody in dealing with others.

***

Junayd: Humility is not being arrogant towards the people of either world and being self-sufficient in God. (TA 445)

ʿAbd Allāh Rāzī: Humility means abandonment of discrimination in service. (RQ 221)

Shiblī: When I asked Yūsuf b. Isbāṭ what the ultimate humility is, he replied, "It is where you come out of the house and see everyone you meet as better than you." (TA 503)

Ibrāhīm Shaybānī: Humility is a form of purifying the inward being, the graces of which are displayed by the outward being. Pride is a form of turbidity of the inward being, the darkness of which appears in the outward being. (TSS 405)

Repentance (*tawba*)

Author: Your existence is a sin to which no other can be

compared. So it is better that you repent from your very existence.

***

Sahl b. ʿAbd Allāh: Repentance means forgetting the sin one has committed. When someone objected that repentance means not forgetting the sin, Sahl replied, “It is not as you view it, because remembering an act of infidelity in the time of fidelity is itself infidelity.” (TA 321)

Ruwaym: Repentance is repenting of repentance. (TA 486)

Abū Bakr Wāsiṭī: Sincere repentance occurs when no trace of transgression remains in the repenter, inwardly or outwardly. Whoever repents sincerely becomes free all the time from fear of any kind. (TA 744)

Junayd: Repentance has three meanings: the first is regret, the second resolution not to repeat, and the third the purging of yourself from iniquities and animosity. (TA 446)

Dhū n-Nūn: Ordinary repentance is from sin, while that of the elect is from heedlessness [of God]. (RQ 27)

Ibn ʿAṭāʾ: Repentance (*tawba*) is of two kinds: that of contrition (*inābat*) and that of merit (*istijābat*). That of contrition refers to one repenting out of fear of God’s punishment. That of merit refers to one repenting out of shame before God's munificence. (RQ 143)

Qushayrī: Repentance is the first of the waystations of the Path. It is the first of the stations of the seekers. The literal meaning of the word *tawba* is 'return'. In the canon law, repentance means returning from what is canonically condemnable to that which is canonically meritorious.

Sunni jurisprudents have stated that there are three conditions for repentance to be accepted:

1. remorse over offenses committed in the past;
2. restraint from error in the present; and
3. resolve not to offend in the future.

These authorities maintain that the very remorse is repentance. (RQ 136)

Abū ʿAlī Ad-Daqqāq: Repentance is of three kinds: the first is repentance itself; the second, contrition; and the third, penitence (*awbat*). Ordinary repentance means repenting through fear of punishment. Contrition means repenting out of craving for merit. Penitence means repenting neither in fear of punishment nor in desire for merit but in adhering to what one is commanded. (RQ 141)

Tustarī: Repentance means ceasing to procrastinate. (RQ 141)

Nūrī: Repentance is where you repent from everything other than God. (RQ 142)

Ḥaddād: The devotee has nothing to do with repentance, for it comes to him, not from him. (RQ 144)

Rābiʿa (on being asked by a man if God would forgive him if he repented): No, but if God grants you repentance, then you will repent. (RQ 144)

Maḥfūẓ b. Maḥmūd: A truly repentant person is someone who repents for both his corrupt acts and his acts of obedience. (TSS 273)

I repent for not having
kissed the Sāqī's lips; and now
I bite my lip, having
listened to the ignorant.

Ḥāfiẓ

Adherence to Divine Unity (*tawḥīd*) and the Adherent to Divine Unity (*muwaḥḥid*)

Author: Adherence to Divine Unity means effacing the illusory imagination of the multiplicity that stems from the ego in the sea of God's Unity.

***

Junayd: Adherence to Divine Unity is a spiritual reality in which formalities become insignificant, sciences vanish, and God exists as He ever has and ever will. Transitoriness and imperfection cannot approach Him. (TA 446)

Junayd (explaining a matter connected with adherence to Divine Unity and describing those who adhere to Divine Unity): They exist without being and are manifested without manifestation.

Sarrāj's commentary: This means that the adherents to Divine Unity are among things as if the adherents did not exist and appear among things as if the things were not manifest, for their existence among things is through their persons, which are non-existent, whereas their appearance among things is by way of their inner beings. This is the meaning of 'being' and 'manifesting'. (LT 356)

Junayd: The limit of the intellect in grasping Divine Unity is bewilderment. (RQ 514)

Junayd: Adherence to Divine Unity means emergence from the constriction of temporal conventions towards the boundless space of eternity. (MA 196)

Abū Yaʿqūb Nahrajūrī: If one merely imitates adherence to Divine Unity, one is far from the Path. (TSA 342)

ʿAlī b. Sahl Iṣfahānī: Adherence to Divine Unity is close

to subjective notions and far from objective realities. (TSS 236)

Junayd: Adherence to Divine Unity means knowing God's eternalness through the transitory. This means that you know that although a flood is caused by the sea, the flood is not the same as the sea. (TA 442)

Junayd: The ultimate adherence to Divine Unity is denying every Divine Unity. This means that you deny every Divine Unity that you can know, saying "This is not the real Divine Unity." (TA 442)

Junayd: Adherence to Divine Unity is certitude. When asked in what way, he said: "That you know that the motion and rest of the creation is God's action, and no one is a partner to Him. Once you realize this, you have fulfilled the condition of adherence to Divine Unity." (TA 447)

Ruwaym: Adherence to Divine Unity is effacement of the traces of humanness and detachment from the world through God. (TA 486)

Shiblī: Adherence to Divine Unity veils the adherent from the beauty of the Oneness. (TA 631)

Ad-Daqqāq: Adherence to Divine Unity means looking at things through the eye of non-existence. (TA 657)

When Junayd was asked about elect adherence to Divine

Unity, he explained, "This is where the devotee has cast himself before the flow of God's ordainment, such that the dictates of God's power in the seas of God's Divine Unity come upon him through annihilation in God from his *nafs* and from others' appeals to him. At the same time, he experiences God's response through the realities of His Being, and His Unicity in the reality of nearness to Him, through the departure of his corporeal senses and motions and with God's standing by him in what He wants from Him.

This is the final stage of the devotee's state, where it returns to what it was in the beginning, as it was before it came to be. (RQ 515)

Junayd: The Unity by which sufis are distinguished is the separation of the Eternal from the temporal, and the departure from the realms of the *nafs*, by means of abandoning what pleases them and what they do or do not know, such that God takes the place of everything. (RQ 517)

Sarrāj: Shiblī was asked, "Tell us something about Pure Unity singled out by the tongue of the Truth!" He replied, "Woe to you! Whoever answers concerning *tawḥīd* using expressions is a heretic; whoever alludes to Him is a dualist; whoever points to Him is an idolater; whoever speaks about Him is heedless; whoever is silent about Him is ignorant. And whoever thinks that he has reached Him has not gained anything; whoever indicates that he is close to Him is really far away; whoever shows ecstasy through himself has not really experienced it; and whatever is discerned with speculation and perceived with the intellect, in the most perfect of its conceptions, will come back to you, as it is a created thing like yourselves. (RQ 518)

What does it mean to learn about God's Unity?
To burn yourself before the One.
If you want to be lit up like the day,
Burn your night-like self!

Mathnawī

Unity (*tawḥīd*), its Affirmer (*muwaḥḥid*) and the Object of Affirmation (*muwaḥḥad*)

Rūzbihān: If I link Unity to the affirmer (*muwaḥḥid*), then I am saying that it is created. If I say that it belongs only to the Object of Affirmation, then how can anyone seeking it be able to realize it? If I say that it is the relationship between the affirmer of Unity and the One Affirmed, then I have gone as far as I can. That is to say, He transcends any incarnation through temporal forms in related places of similarity.

Tawḥīd, muwaḥḥid and muwaḥḥad are three different things only in name, but in essence they are one. This is beyond words. (SS 533)

The Unity of God (*tawḥīd-i Ḥaqq*) and the Unity of Creation (*tawḥīd-i khalq*)

Ḥallāj: If I say that *tawḥīd* appeared from Him, I will be dividing God's Essence into two.

Rūzbihān: In truth, *tawḥīd* is of two types: the Unity of God (*tawḥīd-i Ḥaqq*) and the unity of creation (*tawḥīd-i khalq*). The unity of creation consists of His Signs (*āyāt*), while the Unity of God consists of His Attributes, and the Attributes are not separate from His Essence. (SS 535)

Trust-in-God (*tawakkul*), Submission (*taslīm*) and Consignment (*tafwiḍ*)

Author: Trust-in-God is relying on God; submission is accepting His will; and consignment is delivering yourself into His hands.

***

Junayd: Trust-in-God is being with God as you were before you came into existence. (TA 445)

Abū Bakr Warrāq: Trust-in-God means using the spiritual moment to its fullest, purged of the impurity of expectation, whereby one has no regret over what has passed nor eagerness over what may come, so that the moment may not be wasted. (TA 538)

Abū ʿAbd Allāh Maghribī: Once, going out into the desert, I met a lad in the bloom of youth without provision or supplies. "Hey, my gallant lad!" I hailed him. "Where are you bound like this with no provision?"

"Look around you," he replied. "Do you see anything apart from God?" (TA 560)

Ibn Khafīf: Trust-in-God means finding sufficiency in what God has provided and not questioning what God has decreed. (TSS 465)

Kharaqānī: The sign of trust-in-God is that lion and dragon, fire, sea and pillow are all five the same to you, for all are one in the realm of Divine Unity. (TA 711)

Ad-Daqqāq: Trust-in-God has three degrees: trust-in-God itself, submission, and consignment. One who trusts in God is at peace with God's promise; the submitted one is satisfied by God's knowledge; and the consigner is content with God's decree. Trust-in-God is the beginning, submission the middle, and consignment the end. (RQ 250)

Ad-Daqqāq: Trust-in-God consists of three stages. The first stage is trust-in-God itself, which is the beginning and an attribute of ordinary people. The second is submission in God, which is the intermediate stage and an attribute of the elect. The third is consignment, which is the end and an attribute of the elect of the elect. (KAM II 330)

A group came to Junayd, seeking provision. "If you know where it is," he told them, "then seek it out."

"We seek it from God," they said.

"If you know that He has forgotten you, then remember Him," said the master.

"We shall go home," they said, "and sit trusting in Him."

"This exercise is based on doubt," said the master.

"Then what is the best strategy?" they asked.

"Abandoning strategies," he replied. (RQ 254)

Abū Yaʿqūb Mazābilī: Trust-in-God means abandoning free will. (TSA 338)

Sahl b. ʿAbd Allāh Tustarī: Trust-in-God means abandonment of mind-control. (TSA 338)

Bishr Ḥāfī: Trust-in-God means contentment. (TSA 338)

Abū Ḥafṣ Ḥaddād: Trust-in-God means disengaging one's own power. (TSA 338)

Ḥallāj: Trust-in-God means seeing the Causer. (TSA 338)

Fatḥ Mawṣilī: Trust-in-God means being weary of secondary causes. (TSA 338)

Shaqīq Balkhī: Trust-in-God means seeing God while in

the helplessness of immersion. (TSA 338)

Shiblī: Trust-in-God means eliminating everyone from the vision of the heart. (TSA 338)

Fuḍayl b. ʿAyāḍ: The reality of trust-in-God is that one has no hope in anything other than God and has no fear of anything other than God. (TA 98)

Jaʿfar Khuldī: Trust-in-God means having no preference between being and nothingness. (KM 197)

Anonymous: Trust-in-God is considering little and much as the same. (RQ 250)

Abū l-Qāsim b. Masrūq: Trust-in-God is turning from what is for you to that which is against you, then turning from what is against you to that which is for God and towards God. (TSS 239)

Abū ʿAmr Nujayd: The one who trusts in God is he who is content with God's decree concerning him. (TSS 239)

It is unbelief on the Path to rely
on piety and knowing how.
Even if the traveler has a hundred techniques,
he must still trust in God.

Ḥāfiẓ

Making Accusations (*tuhmat*)

Author: You must make accusations against your *nafs* to keep it from making ego-based claims and to keep it from being critical of others.

***

Ṭalḥa Nablī: Make accusations in respect of your own actions to know their value, and stop making accusations against others to end the state of war. (TSA 243)

Be thankful you're branded a heretic,
that your ego not stand in the way.
Strive to gain grace of vitality
from love and the spiritual wine.

Ḥāfiẓ

Ambition (*jāh-ṭalabī*)

Author: The ambitious sufi remains a stranger to Divine Unity and the Path.

***

Shaikh Sīrwānī: The final thing which leaves the hearts of the highest sufis is ambition. (TSA 540)

Shaikh Sīrwānī: God gives debasement as a reward to whoever seeks greatness from a worthless path. (TSA 568)

Seek poverty and annihilation
from those who have it.
Don't seek it from those
who are attached to wealth and status.

Maghribī

Determinism and Free Will (*jabr wa ikhtiyār*)

Author: As long as you are you, you enjoy free will. When you are no longer you, determinism prevails and free will is God's. In traveling the path from being to non-being, the wayfarer is between the two.

Masters of the Path have said that if at the beginning of the Path the wayfarer believes in determinism, he is an unbeliever. If at the end of the Path he believes in free will, he is likewise an unbeliever.

This means that at the beginning the sufi should rely on his own efforts, while at the end he should be conscious of God's attraction.

***

Abū Bakr Wāsiṭī: On setting out, the disciple enjoys free will. When he has matured, free will disappears and he sees God's knowledge in his own ignorance, God's existence in his own non-existence, and God's will in his own absence of will. (TA 740)

Concentration and Dispersion (*jamʿ wa tafriqa*)

Author: Concentration means annihilation in Unity, and dispersion means expression of individual being.

***

Junayd: Concentration means nearness to Being, and dispersion means absence from Being through human nature. (TA 443)

Yūsuf b. Isbāṭ: Concentration means centering the heart in gnosis, and dispersion means scattering one's consciousness in states. (TA 505)

Bundār b. Ḥusayn: Concentration is that which is with God, and dispersion is that which is for God. (TA 468)

Ad-Daqqāq: Dispersion is ascribed to you, and concentration is what is taken from you.

Qushayrī's commentary: This means that what one gains through maintaining devoteeship and what one receives in terms of states in a condition of human nature are counted as dispersion, whereas that which comes from God in terms of the appearance of spiritual realities (*maʿānī*), along with Divine Grace and beneficence, is counted as concentration.

These latter are the least of the states which devotees receive in concentration and dispersion, for they take place where one is conscious of one's actions. When God makes someone present to Him in terms of that person's acts, whether in devotion or in oppostion, that person is characterized by dispersion. However, when God makes someone present in terms of His own acts, that person is at the station of concentration.

Dispersion affirms creation, while concentration affirms God. The devotee has no control over whether he is experiencing concentration or dispersion, for when one is not in dispersion, one has no devotional practice, and when one is not in a state of concentration, one has no gnosis. (RQ 103)

Qushayrī: The concentration of concentration is higher than this. Furthermore, there is a difference among people in this context depending on their states and their ranks. When one affirms one's *nafs* and the phenomenal world, yet sees this all as founded in God, one is in a state of concentration. Now when one is taken from awareness of the phenomenal world and of one's *nafs*, becoming completely unconscious of all that is other and unaware of what is apparent through being dominated and overwhelmed by Reality, then one is in a state of the concentration of concentration.

Dispersion means seeing God through other

things. Concentration means seeing other things through God. The concentration of concentration means becoming totally obliterated from all things, and having no sensation of what is other than God while being overwhelmed by Reality.

After this comes a subtle state, which the sufis call the 'second dispersion'. In this state one experiences sobriety whenever one must perform required devotions, so one can perform one's religious obligations at their proper times. This is a return to God through God, not a return to the servant through the servant.

Throughout all these states, one sees oneself being controlled by God, seeing God as the ultimate source of his essence, and God's knowledge and will as the true performer of his actions and the originator of his states. (RQ 105)

Nahrajūrī: Concentration is totally God, where all things are existent through God. Dispersion is an attribute of God shown through the worthless, meaning that whatever is other than God is worthless compared with God and whatever attribute blocks out God is a dispersion. (TA 508)

Wāsiṭī: When you are conscious of God, you are going into a state of concentration. When you are conscious of yourself, you are turning to a state of dispersion. (TA 743)

Wāsiṭī: God turns one towards concentration by His own

knowledge. One goes into dispersion by one's own determination and volition. In reality, concentration is dispersion, and the reverse. (TA 743)

Rūdbārī: Concentration is the inward aspect (*sirr*) of adherence to Divine Unity (*tawḥīd*), and dispersion its outward expression. (TA 756)

Ḥuṣrī: As long as phenomenal being prevails, dispersion obtains. When phenomenal being disappears, God appears. The reality of concentration is being conscious of nothing but God and speaking only of God. (TA 762)

Nūrī: Concentration in God is dispersion in what is other than God. Dispersion from what is other than God is concentration in God. (KM 165)

Rūzbihān: Concentration is Eternity Itself without non-being. Concentration occurs when God concentrates mysteries in the heart of the gnostic in the guise of lights. (SS 563)

Chivalry (*jawānmardī* or *futuwwat*)

Author: Chivalry is giving priority to others over yourself in every matter and being at the service of others with heart and soul, such that you are unaware of benefit or loss to yourself.

***

Ad-Daqqāq: Chivalry is taking action for the sake of others. (TA 656)

Ḥārith Muḥāsibī: Chivalry is giving justice and not expecting it in return. (TA 355)

Kharaqānī: Chivalry is an ocean with three sources: generosity, kindness, and having no need for creation while being in need of God alone. (TA 695)

Kharaqānī: (on being asked how a chivalrous person knows that he is chivalrous): If God grants a thousand miracles (*karāmāt*) to his brother and just one to him, he would still take that single miracle and add it to the thousand his brother has already been granted. (TA 710)

Junayd: Chivalry is bearing the burden of others and giving generously of whatever you have. (TA 445)

Abū l-Qāsim Muqrī: Chivalry means seeing the virtues of others and the deficiencies of yourself. (TSS 511)

A man was planning to get married, but before his prospective bride arrived, she fell ill with small pox and one of her eyes was damaged. When the man heard this, he said that he experienced pain in his own eye and had gone blind. The bride was brought to his house as planned and they lived together for twenty years.

When the wife died, the man opened his eyes. When asked what had happened, he explained that he had pretended to be blind so as not to upset her. The others exclaimed that he was the most chivalrous of anyone. (RQ 359)

Shiblī: Chivalry is wanting for others not just what you want for yourself but even more. (TA 634)

Qaṣṣāb: The chivalrous are those who bring comfort to others because they are in the company of God, not others. They look at others from the perspective of God. (TA 642)

Ḥamdūn Qaṣṣār: When I was passing through Nishapur, a wanderer, named Nūḥ, who was famous for his chivalry approached me. I hailed him and asked him the meaning of chivalry.

"Do you mean my chivalry," he asked, "or yours?"

"Both," I replied.

"Mine," he said, "is where I take off my ordinary cloak and put on a patched one, going through what the patched-cloak wearers do, until I become a sufi. Out of shame before others because of this dress, I avoid committing sins. Now your chivalry is where you take off the patched cloak, so that you will deceive no one and no one will deceive you. My chivalry is preservation of the law (*sharīʿat*), and yours is preservation of Reality (*ḥaqīqat*)." (TA 401)

Kharaqānī: The sages see God by the light in their hearts, the friends of God by the light of certitude, and the chivalrous by the light of direct vision. (TA 698)

Karkhī: The chivalrous have three signs: unfailing fidelity, unremitting praise, and unsought-for bestowal. (KM 141)

Makkī: Chivalry means overlooking the faults of one's brethren. (TSS 202)

Būshanjī: Chivalry means good conduct, constant meditation, and not seeing with your self anything which your inward conscience is opposed to. (TSS 461)

Muḥammad ash-Shubhī: Chivalry means being good-natured and being good to others. (TSS 506)

There was a man who claimed to be chivalrous. A group of chevaliers paid him a visit. The man ordered his servant to lay out the meal-cloth. He repeated the command two or three times, but the servant did not bring the cloth.

Looking at each other, the guests said, "Chivalry does not involve employing someone that you have to call several times for the meal-cloth to be brought."

When the servant finally brought the cloth, the man demanded to know why he had not brought it sooner.

The servant replied that ants had gotten into the folded cloth. "It would not have been chivalrous," he said, "to have laid it out before the guests with ants on it, and it wouldn't have been chivalrous to throw the ants off it. I stood waiting till they had left it themselves. Then I brought the cloth."

The guests all praised him, saying, "It is you who have the right to serve us." (RQ 362)

Sulamī told me that Naṣrābādī was told many times that his disciple, ʿAlī, the cantor of the *khānaqāh* [the sufi's gathering place] would get drunk at night, then would attend the master's meetings in the daytime. The master never responded to what he was being told until one day it happened that he went out with one of the disciples who had made this accusation.

They encountered ʿAlī the cantor, lying on the ground where he had fallen in a drunken stupor, his mouth dirty.

"How many times do I have to tell your good self that ʿAlī has fallen into a condition like this?" asked the disciple.

The master gave him a stern look and told him, "Turn him over and carry him over your shoulders to his home."

The disciple had to do as he was told. (RQ 365)

A pilgrim went to sleep in Medina. When he woke up, he thought his money-belt had been stolen. He rushed out and encountered Imām Jaʿfar Ṣādiq and accused him of stealing the money-belt.

When the Imam asked how much was in it, the pilgrim replied, "A thousand dinars."

The Imam invited him to his home and gave him a thousand dinars. When the man went back, he found the money-belt right where he had left it. Full of shame, he dashed over to the Imam's house to give him back the thousand dinars.

Refusing it, the Imam said, “I cannot take back what I have given.”

When the man asked others who the man was, he was told that it was the well-known Imam. (RQ 363)

When Shaqīq Balkhī asked Imām Jaʿfar Ṣādiq about chivalry, the latter countered, “What do you think it is?”

“If we are given something,” Shaqīq replied, “we give thanks, and if nothing is given, we are patient.”

“The dogs of Medina are thus,” said the Imam.

When Shaqīq asked the Imam what his view of chivalry was, the latter stated, “If we are given something, we give it to someone else, and if nothing is given, we are patient.” (RQ 363)

Three persons were praying in a ruined mosque. While they slept, Ibrahīm Adham stood at the door. When they asked why he had done that, he explained, “The weather was very cold and the wind bitter. I planted myself by the door, so that you wouldn’t suffer too much, so that I would take the brunt of it.” (TA 114)

One day Abū Saʿīd Abī l-Khayr was out walking in the Nishapur marketplace with a group of his disciples. As soon as they entered the marketplace, they encountered a group of naked youths, wearing leather slippers and carrying a man on their shoulders.

When they came up to the master, he asked, “Who is this man?”

“The chief of the gamblers,” they replied.

"Why do you consider him a chief?" asked the master.

"Because he lost everything he had," they said.

Hearing this, the master gave a cry and declared, "Be a gambler who loses all and thus becomes a chief!" (AT 231)

Once during his stay in Nishapur, Abū Saʿīd visited the public bath, where a dervish set to scraping the dust off his body after the first bathing. Whatever dirt he took from the master's back, the dervish collected on his arm, so that the master could see the dirt that was being removed.

In the course of his work the dervish asked the master the meaning of chivalry. The master replied, "Not showing the customer to his face the dirt one has removed." (AT 280)

When Abū Ḥafṣ Ḥaddād arrived in Baghdad, the sufi elders of the city gathered round him, asking him about chivalry. He countered by asking what they thought it meant.

"In my view," said Junayd, "chivalry is not seeing one's own chivalry and not ascribing to oneself whatever one does, not claiming, 'I did this.'"

"That is well said," declared Abū Ḥafṣ, "but in my view it is dealing fairly and not expecting fairness in return."

Junayd turned to the others and told them, "Put this into practice, my comrades!"

"It is not enough to talk about this," added

Abū Ḥafṣ.

Hearing this, Junayd exhorted his companions to rise and get into action, exclaiming, "Abū Ḥafṣ has outdone Adam and his descendants in chivalry!"

ʿAṭṭār's commentary: This means that he stretched the limits of what humankind could attain in terms of chivalry to a new level. (TA 394)

Manliness and chivalry
are the principles of our Path;
The souls of monarchs are alive
in the precincts of our court.

Sanāʾī

Generosity (*jūd*), Liberality (*sakhā*) and Meanness (*bukhl*)

Author: Generosity and liberality are attributes of the liberated and the chivalrous, while meanness is an attribute of the selfish and egocentric.

***

Ad-Daqqāq: Liberality is not where a rich person gives something away. It is where an empty-handed person gives of one's nothingness to a rich person. (RQ 416)

Anonymous: Generosity means responding nobly upon

one's first impulse. (RQ 406)

Bishr b. Ḥārith: In staring upon a stingy person, the heart hardens. (RQ 408)

Need (*ḥājat*)

Author: Need is in the domain of the ego. One without ego has no need of anyone.

***

Abū Turāb Nakhshabī (on being asked, "Do have any need of us?"): How could I have need of you or anyone like you, when I have no need of God Himself?"

ʿAṭṭār's commentary: This means that he was at the station of contentment. So what does the contented one have to do with need?

The luminous interior of the Beloved
is the world-revealing goblet.
What need is there
to express one's needs there?

Ḥāfiẓ

State and Station (*ḥāl wa maqām*)

Author: A state is an infusion (*wārid*) from the realm of Unity which frees the sufi from ego-ness for a time.

***

The sufis consider a state to be a spiritual reality (*maʿnā*) which enters the heart without the input of any effort or eliciting on the sufi's part. It may involve an experience of joy or sorrow, of expansion or contraction, of yearning, of awe or of excitment. States are bestowed, while stations are obtained. States represent generosity itself, while stations represent the reward for striving. One who enjoys a station is fixed in that station, while one who experiences a state may go higher. (RQ 92)

Junayd: A state is something which may descend upon the heart, though not lasting. (TA 445)

Abū l-Ḥasan Ṣāʾigh: States come on like bolts of lightning. If they last, this is an experience of the *nafs* and an adjustment back to one's material nature. (TSS 315)

Ruwaym: A sufi experiences neither states nor stations, for the sufi has passed beyond them. (TbA 264)

Abū l-Khayr Aqṭaʿ: When one makes one's actions apparent, one is ostentatious, and when one makes one's state apparent, one is making claims. (TSA 471)

Qushayrī: A station is what the devotee arrives at through seeking, striving and effort. The station of each person is where he stands in relation to this and in relation to his self-discipline. The condition is that one cannot advance from one station to another until one has satisfied the requirements of the given station. One cannot properly experience a station without being completely aware of God's placing one in that station. (RQ 91)

The Pilgrimage and Visitation of the Kaʿba (*ḥajj wa ziyārat-i kaʿba*)

Author: The true Pilgrimage for the sufis is visitation of the Owner of the house, not the house itself.

***

They saw Shiblī running with a flame in the palm of his hand. When they asked him where he was going, he said, "I'm running to set the Kaʿba on fire, so people will focus on the God of the Kaʿba." (TA 617)

Muḥammad b. Faḍl: I am amazed that one can cross deserts by one's own will to arrive at His house and make visitation thereof and view the relics of His Prophet. Why not take steps by one's own will to reach one's heart to see the signs of one's own Lord? (RQ 57 and TA 519)

Naṣrābādī performed the Pilgrimage forty times with trust-in-God (*tawakkul*). Then he saw a dog emaciated from hunger and thirst but had nothing to feed it with.

He asked who would be willing to buy the merit of forty Pilgrimages for a piece of bread. A man came forward and made the purchase, getting a receipt in return, and the master gave the piece of bread to the dog.

A visionary saw what had occurred and, emerging from his meditation corner, jabbed the master with his fist.

"You wretch," he exclaimed, "so you think you did something, giving the merit of forty Pilgrimages for a piece of bread? My father [Adam] sold paradise for a couple of grains of wheat, while that piece of bread was made up of over a thousand of such grains!"

When the master heard this, he went over to a corner and bowed down his head in shame. (TA 788)

Qaṣṣab: The Devil has already been slain by God. It is not chivalry to stone what has already been killed by one's Lord. (This is a reference to the rite of stoning the Devil in the course of the Pilgrimage.) (TA 643)

When a man came to see Junayd, the master asked where he was coming from. When told that he had been on the Pilgrimage, Junayd asked if he had performed all the rites. When the man said that he had, Junayd asked, "When you first left the house and set out from your country, did you vow to take leave of all your transgressions?"

When the man answered, "No," Junayd said, "Then you did not truly depart."

Then Junayd asked, "When you passed from stage to stage on the journey, did you do so through God?"

When the man replied, "No," Junayd said, "Then you did not truly alight at each stage."

Then Junayd asked, "When you donned the sacred dress (*iḥrām*) at the appointed spot, did you leave off the attributes of human nature along with your daily clothes?"

When the man answered, "No," Junayd said, "Then you did not truly don the sacred dress."

Then Junayd asked, "When you stopped on the hill of ʿArafāt, did you experience the visionary revelations of that spot?"

When the man replied, "No," Junayd said, "Then you did not truly stand on ʿArafat."

Then Junayd asked, "When you arrived at Muzdalifa, attaining your desire, did you abandon all your personal desires?"

When the man said, "No," Junayd said, "Then you did not truly arrive at Muzdalifa."

Then Junayd asked, "When you performed the circumambulation of the Kaʿba, did you experience the inward house as the site of transcendance of the subtleties of the plane of the Divine Beauty?"

When the man answered, "No," Junayd said, "Then you did not truly perform the circumambulation."

Then Junayd asked, "When you did the Run between Ṣafāʾ and Marwa, did you perceive the station of the former and the degree of the latter?"

When the man replied, "No," Junayd said, "Then you did not truly perform the Run."

Then Junayd asked, "When you reached Minā, did your ego-impulses abate?"

When the man answered, "No," Junayd said, "Then you did not truly reach Minā."

Then Junayd asked, "When you made the sacrifice at the slaughtering place, did you sacrifice all your *nafs'* desires?"

When the man replied, "No," Junayd said, "Then you did not truly perform the sacrifice."

Then Junayd asked, "When you threw the stones, did each stone you threw speak to you of its meaning?"

When the man answered, "No," Junayd said, "Then you truly threw no stone and, indeed, did not perform the Pilgrimage at all. Go back and do the Pilgrimage in this manner, that you may attain the station of Abraham." (KM 425)

The pilgrims all arrived so solemnly,
Grateful for mercy from Compassionate God
And weary of the trials of the Hijāz,
Rescued from hell and its most painful torment.
They went to Mecca then from ʿArafāt,
Each pilgrim shouting, "Here I am!" while there.
Once they'd completed there the pilgrimage,
They turned towards the safety of their homes.
I spent some time in welcoming them back,
Offering myself sincerely at their service,

And in that caravan which had arrived
Was a dear friend who was both good and noble.
I asked him, "Now that you have finally been
Relieved of all the trials of traveling,
Which kept me feeling left behind back here,
Thinking of you, as your concerned close friend,
I'm happy that you made the pilgrimage,
For there is no one like you in this region.
Tell me: how did you show deep reverence
Worthy of that Almighty Sacred Lord?
And when you put the pilgrimage garb on,
What goal did you pronounce as your intention?
Did you prohibit for yourself from then on
Everything other than Eternal God?"
He answered, "No." I said, "Did you cry out
'Here I am!' with both knowledge and respect?
And did you hear God's voice come in reply,
Then turn to Him the way that Moses did?"
He answered, "No." I said, "When slaughtering
A sheep for orphans and the destitute,
Did you have His proximity as your aim,
While slaying at the same time your cursed self?"
He answered, "No." I said, "When you went in
The Sanctuary like those saved in the cave,
Were you protected from your own self's evil
And from the pain of exile and hell's torment?"
He answered, "No." I said, "When you threw stones
At the three walls that represent the devil,
Did you cast out completely from inside
All blameworthy acts and all established habits?"
He answered, "No." I said, "When you became

Aware of Abraham's high station there,
Did you submit your self sincerely too
With full conviction and true certainty?"
He answered, "No." I said, "Did your run wildly
When circumambulating, like a villain?
Or, while you walked around, did you recall
The angels all assembled near God's Throne?"
He said, "No." I said, "When you would run
Between Ṣafā and Marwa, those two hillocks,
Did you see the two worlds in your pure soul
And did your heart escape from heaven and hell?"
He answered, "No." I said, "When you were kept
Far from the Kaʿba's stone, with a wounded heart,
Did you feel ready then to finally lie
Inside your grave just like a rotting corpse?"
He said, "All of these things which you have said
I hadn't ever thought about before."
I said, "You've gone to Mecca and returned,
But you've bought just the desert's trials through' this;
If you desire to make a pilgrimage
In future, do as I've been teaching you."

DNK

Don't be sanctimonious with me,
O Champion of the Pilgrimage.
You see a house, while I
Observe the House of God.

Ḥāfiẓ

Someone sought counsel from Bishr Ḥāfī, saying, "I have two thousand licit dirhams, and I want to go on the Pilgrimage."

"You are going only as an observer," said the master. "If you are going for the sake of making God content, you should loan something to several paupers, or give something to an orphan or a person with a large family responsibility, to provide their hearts some relief. This is nobler than a hundred Pilgrimages."

"I would really like to go on the Pilgrimage," said the other.

"Because you did not obtain these funds by favorable means, you will not rest until you spend them in an approved way." (TA 133)

Kharaqānī (to a would-be pilgrim): Where are you going?
The pilgrim: To the Hijaz.
Kharāqānī: What are you going to do there?
The pilgrim: I'm going to seek God.
Kharaqānī: Where is the God of Khorasan [the region where they were] that you have to go to the Hijaz? (TA 702)

Bāyazīd: Pilgrims circumambulate the House with their bodies, seeking survival in the world, while lovers circumambulate the Throne with their hearts, seeking encounter with God. (TA 193)

Kharaqānī: Some of God's creatures circumambulate the Kaʿba and some the heaven of the Cultivated House and some around the Throne. The chivalrous ones circumambulate God's Oneness. (TA 690)

The merit of fasting and Pilgrimage
was earned by the person who
performed his pilgrimage
to the dust of the wineshop of love.

Ḥāfiẓ

Veil (*ḥijāb*)

Author: The veil is the obstacle standing between God and the devotee. In Sufi terminology, your existence is your veil between you and God.

***

Dhū n-Nūn: The hardest of veils is being aware of one's *nafs*. (TA 148)

Dhū n-Nūn: God does not hold the devotee dear (*ʿazīz*) in the heights of His Preciousness (*ʿizz*) any more than by displaying the baseness of his *nafs* before Him; nor does He hold in contempt the devotee in the depths of His condemnation any more than by veiling him to the point where he does not see the baseness of his *nafs*. (TA 149)

Hujwīrī: There are two veils: corrosion (*rayn*), which is

never lifted, and beclouding (*ghayn*), which is attributive and may be lifted in time. Corrosion refers to the essence of the individual being a veil before God. (KM 5)

Between lover and Beloved
there is no obstacle.
You are your own veil, Ḥāfiẓ.
Get out from in between!

Ḥāfiẓ

Freedom (*ḥurriyat*)

Author: Freedom is being free of everything but God in both worlds.

***

Qushayrī: Freedom is the emergence of the individual from enslavement to all created things. Anything which is other than God has no access to his heart. The sign of freedom's actualization is the elimination of discrimination between things from his heart, where noble and base are the same to him. (RQ 342)

Ḥallāj: If someone wants to attain freedom, tell him, "Go enslave yourself to devoteeship." (RQ 343)

Presence and Absence (*ḥuḍūr wa ghaybat*)

Author: Presence means being absent from everything but God and present with God. Absence means being present with God and absent from everything else.

***

ʿAlī b. Sahl Iṣfahānī: Presence with God is higher than certitude about God because presence is with the heart. There can be no heedlessness therein. Certitude, however, is an awareness which comes and goes. Those who are present are in the throne-room of God, while those who are certain are in the antechamber. (TA 544)

Ruwaym: Those who are present fall into three categories:

1. those who witness the threat, and are in a state of awe;
2. those who witness the promise, and are in a constant state of hope; and
3. those who witness God, and are in a constant state of rapture. (TA 485)

Rūzbihān: Presence means the presence of the inner consciousness (*sirr*) in the witnessing-place of the Unseen, viewing God manifested in lights. (SS 552)

Rūzbihān: Absence is that of the heart from the phenomenal world through vision of God. Absence of the intellect is from phenomena through witnessing God. Absence of the *nafs* involves its becoming broken by moral conduct with respect to pleasure and passions. Absence of the spirit is in God from God. Absence of the inner conscioiusness (*sirr*) is from the experience of gnosis in the Ultimate Eternal. (SS 551)

Qushayrī: Absence means absence of the heart from knowledge of what is going on in terms of the states of others. One may also become absent from oneself and other things through a prompting which makes one aware of reward and punishment. (RQ 109)

Qushayrī: Presence means presence with God, given that when one becomes absent from the phenomenal world one becomes present with God. One is present with God when one is conscious of being present due to one's being overwhelmed by the remembrance (*dhikr*) of God until one is totally present in one's heart with God. One is present with God to the extent of one's absence from the phenomenal world. If one is totally absent from the phenomenal world, one is totally present with God. When one says that so-and-so is present, one means that the person is present with God in heart and is not heedless. He is constantly conscious of God in his heart. Thereby his visionary revelation (*kashf*) is according to the level at which God conveys spiritual realities (*maʿānī*) specifically to him.

One is also said to be present when one experiences life through the senses or through states of the *nafs* or through states of the phenomenal world.

That is to say that one has emerged from absence and returned to consciousness of the phenomenal world.

Masters have different views of absence, saying that one's absence may be long or short or lasting or not.

Dhū n-Nūn sent someone to Bāyazīd to ask about him and to find out what state he was in. When the man arrived in Basṭām, he asked directions and found the master's house. Answering the door, the master asked what he wanted.

"I am looking for Bāyazīd," said the visitor.

"Who is he?" asked the master. "It's a long time that I've been looking for him."

The visitor came away thinking that the master was crazy. Returning to Dhū n-Nūn, he told him what state he had found the master in.

Dhū n-Nūn wept and said, "My brother Bayazīd has joined his spiritual companions with God." (RQ 111)

Have you ever heard of one
who is present yet absent?
Though I'm among the crowd,
my heart is elsewhere.

Saʿdī

God or the Truth (*Ḥaqq*)

Author: God is said to be Absolute Being.

***

One day a materialist visited the circle of Abū l-Ḥusayn Nūrī, who was speaking about God at the time. The materialist asked him what he meant by 'God'?

"The One," replied the master, "Who adorns the world with all sorts of corruption, yet remains pure Himself." (AT 254)

ʿAlī b. Bundār Ṣirafī: God is a lofty affair which everyone seeks, for finding God means throwing away the world and the hereafter. (TSS 504)

Abū l-ʿAbbās Sayyārī: Only those who are veiled speak of God. (TA 778)

One day a man visiting Abū Saʿīd said, "O Master, I have come for you to show me something of God."

"Come back tomorrow," said the master.

When the man left, the master told his disciples that before the man came back, they should catch a mouse, put it in a box, and close the box tight.

When the man returned, he held the master to his promise. The master said for the box to be given to the man, telling him, "Be careful. Don't open the box!"

The man took the box and went home. Wondering what secret was in the box, the man got all worked up. He could not contain himself. He had to open the box. When he did, the mouse popped out and ran away. The man went back to the master and complained that he had sought the mystery of God from him, but all he was given was a mouse.

"O dervish!" said the master, "I gave you the

mouse in a box. You couldn't keep it hidden. If I were to tell the secret of God, how could you keep it!" (AT 213)

Truth and Falsity (*ḥaqq wa bāṭil*)

Author: The domain of the sufi transcends truth and falsity.

***

Qaṣṣāb: The call of the hundred and twenty-some thousand prophets is the truth, but in phenomenal form. When Reality (*Ḥaqīqat*) appears, neither truth nor falsity remains. (TA 623)

Ḥaddād: When I came to know God, neither truth nor falsity appeared in my heart. (TSA 636)

When you see the truth,
you see nothing but God.
Those who see false things see
what is other than God.

Maghribī

Wisdom (*ḥikmat*)

Author: Wisdom means awareness of some of the realities of the realm of existence and phenomenal beings, and the sage (*ḥakīm*) guides others with perception and benevolence according to their understanding.

***

Junayd (on being asked who can be considered a fair dispenser of wisdom): One who can explain all that is necessary in a few words and give easily understood signs, not finding anything difficult because the knowledge is readily available to him. (HyA 262)

Junayd (on being asked where the dispensing of wisdom is appropriate): The dispensing of wisdom is appropriate wherever the effect of it is welcome to others, the declaring of it is good for everyone, and there is little danger of harmful consequences from it. (JNr 191)

Ḥallāj: Wisdom is an arrow, the believer's heart the target and God the Bowman, and this arrow is never in error. (TfA II 233)

Tirmidhī: Wisdom is the heart's awareness of God's mysteries. (TSA 311)

Abū Bakr Warrāq: The cleric is lower than what he says; the sage is equal to what he says; and the realized gnostic is higher than what he says. (TSA 317)

Abū Ṭayyib Marāghī: Reason is based on logic, wisdom on intimation, and gnosis on evidence. Reason shows the way, wisdom gives indications, and gnosis gives testimony that pure-hearted devotional practice can come only from pure-hearted adherence to Divine Unity (*tawḥīd*). (RQ 15)

Anṣārī: Most people speculate on what will be, while the sage is engaged in what has been. (TSA 324)

Manṣūr b. ʿAmmār: Wisdom speaks in the hearts of gnostics with the tongue of authentication, in the hearts of ascetics with the tongue of elevation, in the hearts of worshippers with the tongue of beatification, in the hearts of disciples with the tongue of meditation, and in the hearts of clerics with the tongue of evocation. (TA 407)

Ḥuṣrī: Until all name and form is cut away with the sword of rejection and you clear the plain of the heart of all that is caused and known, the wellsprings of wisdom will not surge up from the depths of your heart. (TA 761)

Abū ʿUthmān Maghribī: Wisdom is expressed in speech through God. (TSS 483)

Shame (*ḥayā*)

Author: Shame is to feel ashamed at manifesting one's own existence before the Absolute Existence.

***

Tustarī: Shame is higher than fear, for it belongs to the elect, while fear belongs to the clerics. (TA 318)

Junayd: Shame means being conscious of bounties and being aware of one's faults. This combination produces shame. (TA 445)

Abū Bakr Kattānī: Devotional practice has seventy-two parts. Seventy-one of them involve shame before God.

Eternal Life (*ḥayāt-i abad*)

Author: When you die from yourself, you come to live in God, finding eternal life.

***

Ibn ʿAṭāʾ: God has devotees who have realized Union with God and whose eyes are brightened by Him till post-eternity. They have life only through Him. In Union their hearts are with Him, gazing constantly at Him in the purity of certitude, for their lives are integrated with His life. Thus, till post-eternity they have no death. (TA 493)

Perplexity (*ḥayrat*) and Bewilderment (*taḥayyur*)

Author: Since the way to God has no end, whoever comes nearer to God becomes ever more bewildered.

***

Kharaqānī: Bewilderment is like a bird leaving its nest in search of grain but finding none, then losing its way home. (TA 703)

There remained neither Union
nor the one in Union
where imagination
fell into bewilderment.

Ḥāfiẓ

Silence (*khāmūshī*)

Author: The sufi has nothing to say of himself. So in Sufism the important principle is silence. It has been said that whatever can be said is not Sufism. It is also said that silence is the tongue of wisdom.

***

Abū ʿUthmān Ḥīrī: Our principle on this Path is silence and being satisfied with knowledge of God. (TA 480)

Shaqīq Balkhī: There are ten parts of devotional practice: nine involve fleeing from the phenomenal world, and the tenth is silence. (TA 237)

Abū Bakr Fārsī (when asked about the silence of the inner consciousness): Being busy with not existing in past and future. (RQ 184)

Bāyazīd: All this talk and busy-ness and noise and motion and desire lie outside the veil. Inside the veil lie silence and quiet and calm and awe. It takes some audacity to keep oneself absent from the presence of God and in love with oneself. When presence [with God] appears, what need is there for speech? (TA 194)

Be silent, Ḥafiz. These words
are like pure gold. Hold on to them,
for the money-changer is
the counterfeiter of the town.

Ḥāfiẓ

God-cognition (*khudā-shināsī*)

Author: The farther you go from yourself, the closer you come to God.

***

Turughbudi: The only means by which one can reach God is through God Himself, for there is no way to God but God. (TA 558)

Tirmidhī: You want to know God with your *nafs* intact, but your *nafs* does not even know itself, nor can it ever. How could it ever know God? (TA 532)

Bāyazīd (on being asked, the way to God): If you get up out of the way, you will reach God. (TA 198)

Abū Saʿīd Kharrāz: Once I encountered a youth by the sea, wearing a patched cloak, with a bag slung over his shoulder. I thought to myself that though his face was open, his activity was not so obvious. On first sight I thought that he was a realized one, but when I noticed the bag, I judged he might be a seminary student. So I decided to ask him which he was.

"Young man!" I hailed him. "What is the way to God?"

"It is twofold," he replied, "that of the elect and that of the ordinary. You have no idea of the way of the elect. However, the way of the ordinary is the one you are following. You consider your spiritual practice to be the means to get you to God, while you consider the bag to indicate a veil." (TA 459)

Hallāj: The way to God involves but two steps for one to arrive. Take one step away from the world and one from the hereafter, and you will reach God. (TA 588)

Abū l-ʿAbbās Qaṣṣāb: If you were someone seeking God by means other than God, then you would see two Gods. Only God can seek God; and only God can find God, and only God knows God. (TA 643)

Kharaqānī: Some people declare: "God and bread." Others put it the other way round. I say, "God without bread; God without water; God without anything else." (TA 687)

Kharaqānī: This is the way of the fearless and of the crazy and the drunk. To be drunk and crazy and fearless with God is beneficial. (TA 704)

Kharaqānī: When one is absent, everyone talks about one. When one is present, no one can say anything. (TA 700)

Muḥammad b. Wāsiʿ: I have never looked at anything without seeing God therein. (KM 112)

Kharaqānī: Beholding God means seeing nothing but Him. (AAK 83)

Ḥallāj (when asked by someone, what is the way to God): A way is a relationship between two things or two persons. Once what is other than God ceases to exist, what is there left of a 'way'? (JTI 139)

The master, Abū Saᶜīd b. Abī l-Khayr, was in a state of contraction one day when he set out from Mayhana to Sarakhs, as was his custom. Arriving in Dastgird, he encountered Luqmān Sarakhsī, who asked him where he was going.

"My heart is contracted," replied Abū Saᶜīd, "and I am on my way to Sarakhs."

"When you reach Sarakhs," said Luqmān, "give my greetings to the God of Sarakhs!" This was his ironic way of alluding to the fact that God is everywhere and there is no need to move from one place to another to see Him. (AT 239)

Service (*khidmat bi khalq*)

Author: By observing devotion to God you are serving yourself, whereas by serving others you make God content. This is why sufi masters consider the fundamental spiritual practice to be service to others.

***

Spiritual practice
means service to others.

does not mean rosary,
prayer-carpet or cloak.

Saʿdī

One day Abū Saʿīd b. Abī l-Khayr was addressing an assembly in Nishapur, in the course of which he declared, "The *khānaqāh* from top to bottom is filled with jewels, scattered all over. Why don't you pick them up?"

Those assembled all looked around, thinking they would see actual jewels to gather up. When they found nothing, they exclaimed that they saw no jewels.

"Service!" cried the master. "Service!" (AT 226)

Abū Sulaymān Dārānī: When one considers oneself of no value, one misses the sweetness of service. (RQ 221)

Abū Ḥafṣ Ḥaddād: The illumination of bodies is through service, while that of souls is through constancy. (TA 399)

Author: Service to others is a principle of the ancient culture of Iran.

Zoroaster (on his master): The perceptive man was a sage who chose seclusion, abandoning the thinking and intellection of the world, though never forgetting service to others, and working for their aid and benefit. (HKh 38)

Zoroaster: O my God, I wish to bind myself to You with virtuous action and service to others, illuminated by righteousness, beneficence and caring for the deprived and needy. (MzH 231)

Bāyazīd had Mazdean [followers of Zoroaster] neighbors, who had a baby who cried every night at the darkness because the family had no light. Each night the master would carry a lamp over to the neighbors' house, and place it in their house to calm the baby. (TA 176)

Junayd: The sufi cloak has no value; value lies in service. (SkS 171)

Qaṣṣāb would often say: When a disciple sets out to do service in a sufi way, he will be increased in state far more than in doing a hundred rounds (*rakʿat*) of daily prayers (*namāz*); and if he eats a portion less of food, it is better for him than spending all night doing the prayers. (AT 252)

Submissiveness (*khushūʿ*)

Author: Those who become aware of the grandeur of the universe show submissiveness and humility (*tawāḍuʿ*) from the heart before God and phenomenal existents. Submissiveness is a dread in the inward being which affects outward movements in the form of humility.

***

Ḥasan Basrī: Submissiveness is a dread standing in the heart constantly. (TA 46)

A master of the Path: Submissiveness is the heart's standing before God in the fullness of aspiration. (RQ 217)

Junayd: Submissiveness is the keeping of the heart tender before someone fully familiar with the Unseen. (RQ 217)

Anonymous: Submissiveness is a dread which suddenly descends on the heart with visionary revelation (*kashf*) of Reality (*ḥaqīqat*). (RQ 218)

Temperament (*khulq*)

Author: Temperament is a complex of dispositions structuring the behavior and morality of human beings. Good temperament is when someone commits a bad act towards you, you respond with kindness and do not take offense at the harm done to you. Rather, you are joyful. You consider a person who bothers others to be ill, needing to be treated with loving-kindness.

***

Abū Bakr Wāsiṭī: The sublime disposition is where one has animosity towards no one, and no one has animosity towards one, this being the result of the power inherent in the gnosis of God. (RQ 390)

Abū Saʿīd Kharrāz: The sublime disposition is having no aspiration to anything other than God. (TA 462)

Ḥallāj: Temperament means that abuse by others has no effect on you once you have come to know God. (RQ 390)

Kattānī: Sufism is a good temperament. The one with a better disposition is more of a sufi than you. (RQ 390)

Junayd: A good temperament consists of four things: generosity, affection, good counsel, and kindness. (TA 445)

Sarī Saqaṭī: A good temperament is where you neither bother others nor are you bothered by them, having no rancor and seeking no redress. (TA 340)

Abū Saʿīd Kharrāz: Avoid having a bad temperament, as much as you would avoid what is illicit. (TbA 43)

Dhū n-Nūn (on being asked who are the saddest people): Those with the worst temperaments. (RQ 392)

Fuḍayl ʿIyāḍ: I prefer it if a good-natured sinner talks with me than if a bad-tempered pious worshipper does so! (RQ 397)

It is related that Abū 'l-Ḥasan Būshanjī went one day to the house of the sufis. A Turk came out, slapped him and went away. People asked, "Why did you do that? It was Shaikh Abū 'l-Hasan, a great man of the age!" The man felt ashamed and returned to beg forgiveness from the shaikh. The shaikh said, "My friend, rest assured that I did not see this as coming from you, for it came from a place where errors cannot reach." (TA 522)

Abū 'l-Ḥusayn al-Fārsī: Good temperament means three things: to quit complaining to God, to carry out His command with pleasure, and to treat others with kindness as if they are brothers and sisters. (TS 401)

Ibrāhīm Adham (on being asked if he had ever felt pleasure in this world): I felt pleasure just twice. Once I was sitting down and someone came and urinated over me. The other time I was sitting alone and someone came and slapped me. (RQ 393)

People (*khalq*)

Author: People are manifestations of Absolute Being, deserving love and service.

***

Abū Bakr Wāsiṭī: Whatever people have in hand is God's

apportionment and whatever they do is from His wisdom. It is impossible to attain these things by means of a strategem or personal effort. (TA 744)

Abū ʿUthmān Maghribī: People are the forms in which the dictates of the Divine Power flow. (RQ 17)

Fuḍayl b. ʿIyāḍ: The world is an insane asylum and the people therein are the inmates, bound in chains. (TA 97)

Retreat and Seclusion (*khalwat wa ʿuzlat*)

Author: Retreat and seclusion are a matter of your own will. The sufi is surrendered to the Will of God, and the sufi's heart is with Him. Retreat (*khalwat*) and revelation (*jilwat*) are one and the same to such a one.

***

Anṣārī: Retreat means eliminating one's harm to others and looking upon all with love.

When one is beset with the affliction of fullness, one's cure is in emptiness (undertaking retreat). On the other hand, if one is afflicted with the temptation to go into retreat, this is an affliction which must be cured through being replete. Furthermore, if one is liberated from the fortress of chastity, one is afflicted with both emptiness and fullness.

Abū Bakr Qawhī and Abū Bakr Fūrak were debating whether retreat (*khalwat*) is better or company (*khulṭat*). One argued that retreat is better, as long as you do not become empty, while the other asserted that company is better, as long as you do not become involved with others.

It is better that you keep company while remaining in retreat from others in heart and soul. There is no way that an ignorant person is going to undertake seclusion and retreat, only a person who knows, one who is wary and pious.

The best sufis mix with others with dissemblance, remaining alone while among them. (TSA 594)

ʿAbd Allāh Manāzil: Operating under one's own will and gaining something is better than going into retreat and gaining nothing. (TA 542)

Qushayrī: Retreat (*khalwat*) is an attribute of the pure-hearted (*ahl-i ṣafwat*), while seclusion (*ʿuzlat*) is a sign of Union (*wuṣlat*). The beginning disciple has no choice but to undertake seclusion in the early stages by his very nature, whereas at the end one emerges from retreat by becoming realized, that is, gaining intimacy with God.

When the devotee chooses seclusion it is in the belief that it will lead to well-being of temperament, freeing one from the evil of one's self. One does not seek one's well-being as liberation from the evil of others, for the first step is to be aware of the pettiness of one's *nafs* and the second is to see how harmful one is towards others.

When one depreciates oneself, one becomes humble, whereas if one values oneself more highly, one comes to treat others with arrogance.

In reality, seclusion means being separated from blameworthy qualities. Its aim is the transformation of blameworthy attributes into praiseworthy ones, not departure from one's homeland. (RQ 153)

Ad-Daqqāq: Dress the way others do and eat what they eat, but be separate from them in your inner being (*sirr*). (RQ 155)

Ad-Daqqāq: When Shiblī cried, "O people, you're bankrupt! You're bankrupt!", they asked what he meant. He said, "A sign of bankruptcy is being too familiar with others." (RQ 157)

Dhū n-Nūn (on being asked when seclusion is fully achieved): When you achieve seclusion from your *nafs*. (RQ 158)

Passing Thoughts (*khawāṭir*)

Author: Passing thoughts are those which pass into the mind, whether good or bad. One should act on the good ones and forget the bad ones.

***

Qushayrī: Passing thoughts are expressions which enter one's consciousness, whether angelic or diabolical. They may come from the *nafs* or they may come from God. If they are angelic, they represent inspiration; if diabolical, they represent temptation.

If they come from the *nafs*, they are known as stray thoughts (*hawājis*) of the *nafs*. If a thought comes from God, it is known as a thought from God. All these thoughts come as voices.

The truthfulness of the angelic can be confirmed with the corroboration of knowledge. It is said that any passing thought the external aspect of which cannot be authenticated is false. Diabolical thoughts generally lead one to be false and sinful. Those from the *nafs* are considered to follow one's desires and passions, bringing pride and things which are peculiar to the *nafs*. The masters agree that one who eats what is forbidden cannot distinguish between inspiration and temptation. When the passing thoughts of one's *nafs* are silenced, with one's spiritual strivings the eloquence of one's heart speaks, attesting to one's persistence.

A master has said, "Your *nafs* can never speak the truth, and your heart can never lie."

Junayd distinguished between promptings of the *nafs* and Satanic temptations. "Know," he said, "that when the *nafs* pursues something, it persists until it reaches its goal even if it takes a long time. One needs to strive relentlessly with sincerity and persistence.

"Now when Satan tempts, inviting you to lust, when you oppose him, he lets go, turning to tempt you to some other base thing, for all transgressions are the same to him. He is capable of tempting you to any transgression. He has no wish to give preference to one transgression over another."

It has been said that in the case of a passing thought which is angelic, the one experiencing it may either go along with it or oppose it. On the other hand, in the case of a passing thought which comes from God, the devotee never opposes it.

Masters have said that in the case of this latter type two thoughts from God may come at once with one overpowering the other.

Junayd: The one which comes first will be more powerful, because when it occurs, the recipient of it comes to reflect on it as a condition of knowledge.

Ibn ʿAṭāʾ: The second passing thought is stronger, because it is strengthened by the first one.

Ibn Khafīf: The two are the same because both come from God. Neither is greater than the other. The first has no effect on the second because the traces cannot last. (RQ 128)

Fear and Hope (*khawf wa rijā*)

Author: Fear and hope are part of the world of 'I and you'. When there is no ego, there is no fear or hope. Hope is the anticipation of grace and munificence from God.

***

Qushayrī: Fear is a spiritual reality attached to the future, where one fears something undesirable may happen or something pleasant might be denied. This can only happen to someone in the future. The fact is that there is no way that fear can be attached to something in the present. (RQ 189)

Abū Bakr Wāsiṭī: When God appears to the inner consciousness, fear and hope vanish. (TA 743)

Naṣrābādī: Hope leads one to devotional practice, fear distances one from transgression, and meditation shows the way to God. (TA 793)

Qushayrī: Longing differs from hope in that longing produces indolence in the person experiencing it, for he does not follow the path of serious effort, whereas hope is the opposite of this. Hope is worthy, while longing is flawed. (RQ 199)

Ibn Khafīf: Hope means becoming joyful with the presence of God's grace. (RQ 200)

Abū Ḥafṣ Ḥaddād: Fear is God's lash to discipline the one who has bolted from God's antechamber. (RQ 190)

Anonymous: Hope is confidence in the generosity of the Munificent. (RQ 199)

Anonymous: Hope is the beholding of the Divine Majesty in God's Beauty. (RQ 199)

Anonymous: Hope is the nearness of the heart to God's grace. (RQ 199)

Khayr Nassāj: Fear is God's whip, correcting devotees whose disposition has tended to bad behavior. (RQ 70)

Ḥuṣrī: Fear of God is a defect and a veil, for if I am afraid of Him, I still see Him as my aim, while by the same token my hope will not convey me to Him. Thus, in my view the condition of fear and hope is removed for the realized ones, whereas it is incumbent on those who are bound by conventions and sciences to observe etiquette. (TSS 491)

Supplicatory Prayer (*duʿā*)

Author: Prayer means wanting something from God. Certain masters consider this to be an expression of self-existence before God. The sufi who is content with God's will does not pray in supplication.

***

Abū Bakr Wāsiṭī: Whoever accepts fate (*qismat*) as something obtaining since pre-eternity is released from petition and supplication. (TA 746)

ʿAlī b. Aḥmad Būshanjī (on being asked by a man to pray for him): May God protect you from your own troublemaking. (RQ 80)

Anonymous: Silence and total submission in the face of the Divine Command and being content with whatever comes one's way through God's will are the most complete and worthy of qualities. (RQ 438)

Anonymous: The tongues of disciples move with the prayer of supplication, while those of the realized ones are silent. (RQ 448)

ʿAbd Allāh Manāzil: For fifty years I have never uttered a prayer of supplication nor have I wanted anyone to pray for me. (RQ 448)

Some people said: "Pray for me!" A sufi answered: "You are estranged from God because you insist on an intermediary." (RQ 449)

Anṣārī: It is not the practice of sufis to pray in supplication, for they see the command which has come to pass to be that which is for all time. (TSA 323)

Abū ʿAlī ad-Daqqāq: There are three degrees: petition, supplication and praise. The petitioner seeks the world; the supplicator the hereafter; and the praiser God alone. (TA 655)

Bāyazīd (in response when a man asked him to pray for him): O God! They are Your creation, and You are their creator. Who am I in between, to be an intermediary between You and them?

He also said: God is the Knower of one's secrets. Who am I to interfere? (TA 187)

We made the morning prayer in the winehouse.
We submitted the benefit from the prayer on the path to the Beloved.

Ḥāfiẓ

The Heart (*dil*)

Author: When one emerges from the lane of the *nafs* and its desires, one arrives at the city of the heart.

***

Ḥasan Baṣrī (in response to those who asked him what to do, given that their hearts were asleep and his words had no effect on them): If only your hearts were merely asleep, for the sleeper can be shaken awake. Your hearts are dead; however much you shake them, they will not wake up. (TA 33)

Mālik Dīnār: What is the punishment for the wise?
Ḥasan Baṣrī: The death of the heart.
Mālik: What is the death of the heart?
Ḥasan: Love of the world. (TA 37)

Rābiʿa: O Children of Adam! Through the eye there is no journeying to God, nor is there a way to Him through the tongue. The ear is the highway of effort of those who speak, while hand and foot are the rudders of bewilderment. Achievement falls to the heart. Strive, that you may acquire a heart that is awake. Once the heart is awakened, it has no need of the Friend.

ʿAṭṭār's commentary: This means that an awakened heart is one which is lost in God; and if one is lost, what can one do with the Friend? This is what is meant by 'annihilation in God'. (TA 81)

Sahl b. ʿAbd Allāh Tustarī: The *nafs* must die for the heart to become alive. (TA 317)

Kharaqānī: No matter how much devotional practice one may engage in, if one's heart contains anything other than God, one's heart is dead. (TA 697)

Bāyazīd: For forty years I was the watchman of the heart. After forty years I realized that the heart was a polytheist, and its polytheism lay in glancing out of the corner of its eye at what was other than God. (NKAT 94)

The World and the Hereafter (*dunyā wa ākhirat*)

Author: The world and the hereafter are two veils which keep the sufi from God.

***

Junayd: The world is that which descends into the heart and distracts you from God. (HyA X 274)

Fuḍayl b. ʿIyāḍ: Starting off to leave the world is easy, but it is hard to exit from the world completely and leave it behind. (TA 97)

Junayd: If one person possesses the whole world, there may be no harm therein, but if that person's inner being covets so much as a date-stone, there is harm in that. (TA 438)

Aḥmad Ḥuwwārī: The world is like trash, a place for dogs to swarm around. The person who knowingly sits around the world is less than a dog, for the dog seeks out the trash only when it needs food; when it is full, it goes away. (TA 346)

Yaḥyā b. Muʿādh: The whole world from beginning to end is not worth a moment's concern. So how can one spend a lifetime being concerned about the pittance one receives from it? (TA 367)

Abū ʿAbd Allāh Maghribī: I have never seen a dealer more fair than the world. As long as you serve it, it serves you, and as soon as you abandon it, it abandons you likewise. (TA 561)

Abū Isḥāq b. Shahriyār Kāzirūnī: Take remembrance of God with the heart, and the world with the hand. Do not be such that you take remembrance with the tongue and the world with the heart. (TA 868)

Abū Sulaymān Dārānī: Love of the world is the chief of

all sins. (TA 281)

One day Shiblī went out into the desert with his disciples. They came upon a skull on which was inscribed: "Loser of the world and the hereafter."

Becoming ecstatic, Shiblī cried, "By God's Almightiness, this is the head of a saint or a prophet!"

When the disciples asked why he said this, he explained, "You must forfeit everything in the world and the hereafter before you can reach God." (TA 624)

Turūghbudī: Abandoning the world for the sake of the world is a sign of love for the world. (TSS 495)

Bāyazīd: Whenever thought of the world passes through my heart, I do the minor ablution. When thought of the hereafter occurs, I perform the major ablution, for the world is a transitory place (*maḥdath*), and thought of it is unclean (*ḥadath*), while the hereafter is a place of absence, and finding comfort in it is copulation. If one touches something unclean, one must perform the minor ablution, and if one copulates, one must do the major one. (KM 377)

A gnostic fell asleep and
dreamed of the world as a virgin girl.

He asked her, "O maiden, how with all
these husbands you have remained a virgin?"

The world replied, "I'll be straight with you,
Whoever was a man wanted me not.

Just the unmanly wanted me.
That's why I have remained a virgin.

What is the world? Negligence of God.
Not the wealth and women that you have."

Mathnawī

Fortune (*dawlat*)

Author: Fortune belongs to non-existence, and expressing existence is wretchedness.

***

Abū Bakr Wāsiṭī: Fortune comes about in non-being, and damnation in being. (TA 740)

Remembrance (*dhikr*)

Author: The sufi's remembrance means forgetting oneself in remembering God.

***

Junayd: The reality of remembrance is the annihilation of the rememberer in the remembrance. Remembrance obtains when one is contemplating the Remembered. (TA 446)

Kharaqānī: Remembrance is a mercy for the righteous among the ordinary, and heedlessness for the elect. (TA 700)

Abū Saʿīd b. Abī l-Khayr: Remembrance has three aspects. That on the tongue, of which the heart is unaware; this remembrance is a matter of habit. That which is present on the tongue and in the heart; this remembrance is the seeking of merit. That which sets the heart turning, while the tongue falls mute; only God knows the value of this remembrance. (TA 461)

Kharaqānī: Say, 'God!' without caring where you are, 'God!' without desire, 'God!' without anything else. (TA 699)

Abū l-ʿAbbās Dīnawarī: The lowest remembrance is forgetting everything other than the remembrance. The ultimate remembrance is the absence of the rememberer in the remembrance of remembrance. (RQ 82)

Abū l-Qāsim Qushayrī: Remembrance is a fundamental principle on the way of God. No one can reach God without constant remembrance. Remembrance is of two kinds: that of the tongue and that of the heart. The latter comes about only through persistence, where remembrance affects the heart. When the devotee becomes a rememberer in both heart and tongue, he becomes a perfect devotee in the fullest sense in the state of wayfaring on the Path. (RQ 347)

Anonymous: Remembrance of God through the heart is the disciples' sword, which they wield in battle, keeping harm at bay. When an affliction befalls the devotee, he turns in his heart to God, and the affliction is relieved immediately by Him. (RQ 347)

When Junayd was told to say, 'There is no god but God', he replied, "I have not forgotten Him that I should have to recall him again." (RQ 531)

In remembering You
I am so lost from self
that I ask for news of myself
from whomever I meet.

I remembered You so often
that You became me from head to toe;
You approached gradually
and I went away slowly.

One night Bāyazīd came to the *khānaqāh* to sit in remembrance of God. Though he stayed till dawn on the rooftop, he could not bring himself to start remembrance of God. When he recounted this, he was asked why this was so. He explained, "Some words were uttered by my tongue while I was heedless in heart. I recalled this and so I was ashamed before God to remember Him in that state." (RQ 39)

Bāyazīd: Remembrance on the tongue is heedlessness. (TA 144)

Bāyazīd: Remembrance becomes great not through quantity, but rather through presence without heedlessness. (TA 196)

Remembering God
is not everyone's work.
Return to God
is not for any old thug.

Mathnawī

Savor and Imbibing (*dhawq wa shurb*)

Author: Savor appears from the effect of spiritual embellishments and infusions. Inward purity and ongoing infusions lead one to imbibing, whereby one comes to know realities. The continuousness of infusion leads one to satiety, where one forgets oneself before God, and one becomes annihilated through delight.

***

Aḥmad b. ʿAṭāʾ Rūdbārī: Savor is the beginning of ecstasies. When those who are absent imbibe, they become lightheaded, while when those who are present imbibe, they enjoy spiritual relishing (*ʿaysh*). (TSS 498)

Qushayrī: Savor and imbibing are what the sufis experience as the fruit of theophanies and the result of visionary revelations, as well as the appearance of intuitive infusions. Savor precedes, followed by imbibing and then satiety. The purity of their devotional practice makes them taste spiritual realities (*maʿnā*) and the fidelity of their waystations causes imbibing, then the continuity of episodes of Union brings about satiety.

The one who enjoys savor becomes inebriated; the one who imbibes becomes drunk; and the one who is full becomes sober. When one's love is strong, his imbibing is constant. Once this state is continuous, it does not bring on intoxication. If one is sober in God, he becomes annihilated from pleasure. Nothing which comes his way has any effect on him or will alter his state. When one's inner being (*sirr*) becomes pure, his imbibing never becomes darkened. Now when one's imbibing turns to food, it causes him to lose his patient tolerance, so he cannot survive without it.

Yaḥyā b. Muʿādh Rāzī wrote a letter to Bāyazīd, informing him that if there was someone who could drink down a glass and never be thirsty again. The latter wrote back, saying that he was amazed that anyone could be so weak, for there was someone [meaning himself] who could drink up a whole ocean yet remain thirsty, still calling for more.

Know that the cup of nearness comes from the Unseen, but God passes it round only to inner beings which have become liberated from enslavement to things. (RQ 114)

The Path of God (*rāh-i Ḥaqq*)

Author: The beginning of the Path of God is sincerity, and its end is submission.

***

Kharaqānī: The Path is twofold: one way is that of guidance, and the other that of straying. The latter is that of the devotee towards God, while the former is that of God towards the devotee. Thus, if someone claims to have reached God, he has not attained, whereas if someone states that God has taken him to Him, he has truly attained. (TA 697)

Junayd (on being asked how one should follow the Path of God): Abandon the world and you will find the Path. Oppose desires and you will join God. (TA 449)

Kharaqānī: The final stages of the devotee are threefold:

1. one stands facing God, saying, "Allāh";
2. one without self says, "Allāh"; and
3. one says "Allāh" from God to God. (TA 507)

Abū Ḥamza Baghdādī: When one considers that the Path is through God, traveling that Path becomes easy. The way to understanding it is that one has been taught it by God without intermediary.

If one considers the Path to be through reasoning, one wavers between error and correctness. (TA 725)

Abū Bakr Ṭamistānī: There are as many paths to God as there are individuals. (TSS 472)

Ṭamistānī: The Path is for God not towards Him. (TSS 472)

Bāyazīd: The Path of God is like the shining sun. When a person with vision looks with certitude and faith, he sees in every mote, in every particle of every existent, a hundred thousand expressions of the Oneness of God. (KAM IV 302)

Wāsiṭī: The obedient are porters. Porters only bear loads. Now this court is the court of those without longing, the sinners, and the wretched. This domain is that of the bankrupt. (KAM VIII 116)

Mercy (*raḥmat*)

Author: God's mercy encompasses everyone, whether desired or not.

***

When Shiblī was asked if he knew whether God is the Merciful, he replied, "I know that, but ever since I have come to know His mercy, I have never wanted Him to display it towards me." (RQ 343)

Contentment (*riḍā*)

Author: Contentment lies in consigning your volition to God.

***

Abū Ḥāzim Madanī (when asked what his wealth was): My wealth is contentment in God and freedom from need of His creatures. (KM 111)

Junayd: Contentment is the removal of self-will. (TA 445)

Ḥabīb ʿAjamī: Contentment is in a heart free of the dust of hypocrisy. (TA 95)

Bishr Ḥāfī: When I asked Fuḍayl b. ʿIyāḍ whether asceticism or contentment is better, he said, "Contentment, because the contented one never seeks a waystation higher than the one where he already is." (TA 95)

Dhū n-Nūn: Contentment is joy of heart in the bitterness of fate, and the abandonment of self-will before the occurrence of fate, and not seeing fate as bitter when it arrives. Contentment is also the ferment of love in the thick of tribulation. (TA 154)

Abū Sulaymān Dārānī: God has devotees who are ashamed to engage in devotional practice with patience, so they perform their devotions with contentment.

ʿAṭṭār's commentary: 'Patience' here means that 'I myself am patient.' However, this is not at all the case with contentment, where affairs are considered to be the way they are meant to be. Patience is related to you, and contentment to Him. (TA 280)

Abū ʿUthmān Ḥīrī: For forty years God has never put me in a state which I have disliked.

Aṭṭār's commentary: The context is that a repudiator came to invite the master to dinner. The master accompanied the man to his door, whereupon the would-be host cried, "Hey, greedy-gut! The cupboard is bare! Go home!"

The master turned to go back. After he had gone a few paces the man cried, "O master! Come back!"

The master returned, but when he arrived, the man cried, "You take after your ancestors with such an appetite! Go, there is too little here!" The master turned around and headed home again.

This calling and repelling went on a good thirty times, with the master going and coming while displaying not the slightest change in mood. Finally, the man fell prostrate before him, weeping. He repented and became a disciple.

He exclaimed, "What kind of a man are you? I chased you away in the roughest manner thirty times but you did not appear to be affected in the least."

"This was easy," said the master. "Dogs can do this. When you chase them off, they run away. When you call them, they come back, and not a sign of change do they evince. There is nothing to this, where dogs can do as much. The work of men is something else." (TA 477)

Ibrāhīm Ruqqī: The contented one never asks for anything. Overdoing prayers of supplication is not a condition of contentment. (TA 501)

Rābiʿa: The contented person is one who is as joyful in trial as in bounty. (RQ 298)

Bāyazīd: For thirty years I sought to make the Beloved contented. Now for thirty years the Beloved has made me contented. (RSh I 202)

Make me content with what's given;
open the curl on Your forehead,
for the door of volition is not open
to one who still thinks in terms of 'I' and 'you'.

Ḥāfiẓ

The Heart-based Soul (*rūʿ*)

Author: The *rūʿ* represents the fear and hope which gnosis of God brings to the heart of the wayfarer.

***

Cognition of God is in the heart-based soul, which is within the heart. Though finer to the view than the tip of a hair, God fits into the *rūʿ*, while even the very Divine Throne and the atmosphere around it cannot contain Him. (TSA 639)

Hypocrisy (*riyā*)

Author: Whatever you do for the reaction of others is hypocrisy.

***

Abū ʿUthmān Ḥīrī: Outward flouting of the Prophetic Custom is a sign of inward hypocrisy. (TA 480)

Jaʿfar Khuldī: The difference between hypocrisy and sincerity is that the former involves action for the sake of outward appearance, while the latter involves action for the sake of attaining God. (TSS 436)

The hypocrisy of the sanctimonious renunciant

wracked my soul;
Bring the goblet and pour in a potion
to heal this fractured heart.

Ḥāfiẓ

They consider hypocrisy lawful
and the cup of wine unlawful –
How fine the inward Path and creed!
How fine the canon law and doctrine!

Ḥāfiẓ

They've closed the winehouse door.
O Lord! Do not accept it!
For they have opened the door of the house
of hypocrisy and sanctimony.

Ḥāfiẓ

Ascetic Discipline (*riyāḍat*)

Author: Ascetic discipline is the harsh training applied to the *nafs* to make it forget the ego.

***

Ibn Khafīf: Ascetic discipline involves breaking the *nafs*

through service and the prevention of slackness in service. (TSS 464)

Asceticism (*zuhd*) and the Ascetic (*zāhid*)

Author: Asceticism means abandonment of *nafs*-based desires and contempt for the world. The ascetic seeks the blessings of the hereafter or to be close to God. Real asceticism is putting away the world and the hereafter in the face of God's loving-kindness.

***

Ḥallāj: Renouncing the world is asceticism for the *nafs*; renouncing the hereafter, that for the heart; and renouncing oneself is that for the soul. (TA 589)

Abū Sulaymān Dārānī: In God's view the world is less substantial than a mosquito's wing. What value has it that one should reject it in asceticism? (TA 283)

Yaḥyā b. Muᶜādh: The ascetic is outwardly pure and inwardly corrupted, while the gnostic is inwardly pure and outwardly adulterated. (TA 371)

Kharaqānī: I became an ascetic, renouncing everything that was less than God. Then I called myself and heard God answer. (TA 678)

Bāyazīd: Asceticism has no value. I practiced it for three

days, the first day renouncing the world, the second the hereafter, and the third whatever is other than God. (TA 197)

Junayd: Asceticism is the heart's emptiness with respect to whatever the hand is empty of. (RQ 177)

Aḥmad b. Ḥanbal: There are three kinds of asceticism. The first is the renunciation of what is unlawful; this is the asceticism of the ordinary. The second is renunciation of increase in what is lawful; this is the asceticism of the elect. The third is renunciation of everything which distracts you from God; this is the asceticism of the gnostics. (TA 261)

Shiblī: Asceticism is heedlessness, for the world is insignificant and asceticism with respect to what is insignificant is heedlessness. (TA 633)

Sufyān Thawrī: Asceticism in the world is the reduction of expectations. It is not a matter of wearing coarse clothing and eating coarse food. (RQ 175)

Bāyazīd: The gnostic's concern is for the One to Whom he aspires, whereas the asectic's concern is for what he eats. (TSS 74)

Bāyazīd: The ascetic says, "Look what I am doing!" while the gnostic says, "Let us see what God is doing." (NKAT 131)

Shiblī (on being asked who the ascetics were): You are all ascetics with respect to God.

Commentary: This means to say that his listeners had all abandoned God and left Him behind. (JK 376)

Turūghbudī (on being asked the difference between a sufi and an ascetic): The sufi is with his lord while the ascetic is with his *nafs*. (TSS 495)

Intoxication and Sobriety (*sukr wa ṣaḥw*)

Author: After savor (*dhawq*) and imbibing (*shurb*) come intoxication and sobriety. Intoxication comes from a powerful infusion (*wārid*), while sobriety represents awakening of the heart upon the loss, the disappearance, of personal characteristics and habits. As Rūmī puts it:

Once one's soul has become
effaced through one's God,
One departs from intoxication
towards sobriety.

Mathnawī

***

Qushayrī: Sobriety is the return to one's state of self, to

one's own senses and awareness, with one's adjustment after absence. Intoxication itself is a form of absence through a powerful infusion. Intoxication is greater than absence in a certain way, where the intoxicated one is elated. The fact is that in full intoxication the thought of things falls out of one's heart.

This is not a state of 'intoxification', where the infusion is not completed and where one still experiences something of the senses. In this situation the intoxication gains strength, such that it increases absence.

There are many instances where the intoxicated one becomes more complete in absence than the absent one in absence, especially when there is strength in one's intoxication. But there are times when the absent one is more complete in absence than the intoxicated one. There are times when one intentionally tries to be intoxicated. At such times absence is not complete. The absence of devotees is such that it overcomes their hearts, when the devotee experiences visionary revelation, and there is still expectation, anxiety, fear and hope. Intoxication is experienced only by one who has ecstastic states. Such a one gains intoxication when God's beauty is revealed to him making his spirit and heart soar.

When one's intoxication is through God, one's sobriety is as much as one's intoxication, with one's sobriety also being through God. If one's intoxication is mixed with pleasure, one's sobriety is also connected to pleasure. The one who fully realizes intoxication (a *muḥiqq*) is sinless.

From one point of view, intoxication and sobriety both imply distinctions. When awareness of Reality appears, the devotee cries out, overwhelmed by wrath. The devotee in a state of intoxication witnesses the Beauty, while he experiences awareness in a state of sobriety. The devotee in a state of drunkenness is preserved by God's protection—such a one carries out his responsibilities without his own effort.

However, in the state of sobriety one remains self-conscious, carrying out one's responsibilities with conscious effort, by one's own will.

Sobriety and intoxication come after savor and imbibing. (RQ 112)

Audition and Ecstasy (*samāᶜ wa wajd*)

Author: Audition involves the rapture of the sufi who, in the face of love for God, gives up existence, while ecstasy is the harmony of the heart with such rapture.

If you don't have a Beloved,
why not try to find one?
If you have reached the Beloved,
why not be in rapture?

***

Dhū n-Nūn: Ecstasy is a mystery in the heart, while

audition is an infusion by which God ignites the heart, making it zealous in seeking Him. If one listens to it through God, one finds a way to Him, whereas if one listens to it through one's *nafs*, one will fall into heresy. (TA 153)

Junayd: Ecstasy is the cutting off, in joy, of attributes in the presence of the Essence.

ʿAṭṭār's commentary: This means that those attributes which constitute your individuality become severed, while what constitutes your essence within the Unseen becomes manifest. (TA 443)

Junayd: Audition is trouble for the one who makes a point of seeking it, while it is ease of spirit for the one who observes it without effort. (RQ 602)

Abū ʿAlī Rūdbārī: Ecstasy in audition involves the visionary revelation of mysteries through the witnessing of the Beloved. (TA 757)

Nahrajūrī: Audition is a state which manifests through inner burning, taking the devotee back to the ultimate mystery. (RQ 602)

Anonymous: Audition nurtures the spirits of the gnostics. (RQ 602)

Naṣrābādī: Everything has its nourishment, and the nourishment of the spirit is audition. (TA 793)

Abū ʿUthmān Ḥīrī: Audition is of three kinds:

1. That of novices and disciples, appealing for states; they need to be wary of hypocrisy and trouble-making.
2. That of the sincere ones, who seek increase in the intensity of their states; they listen in audition in harmony with the spiritual moment.
3. That of the steadfast gnostics; they have no volition before God concerning what state may come to them governing their motion and rest. (RQ 606)

Qushayrī: Those who engage in audition are of three kinds:

1. The lords of the truth, who converse with God in time of audition.
2. Those who commune with God with their hearts concerning the truth of what they hear; they respond with veracity to what God intimates.
3. Sufis severed from all attachment, distanced from the world and its pestilence, who listen in audition with joy of heart. They are the soundest of all. (RQ 607)

Joy and Sorrow (*shādī wa andūh*)

Author: Sufis are joyful with whatever discomfort or trial comes their way, since they view it as coming from the

Beloved and this is the way God shows attention to them.

Pain and sorrow come
from the Beloved;
I'm joyful that through pain
He's remembering me.

***

Shiblī: When one knows God, one never experiences sorrow.

He also said: Joy in God is better than sorrow before God's face. (TSS 343)

By Ḥāfiẓ's decree:

If there's profit in this bazaar,
it's with the contented dervish.
O Lord, give me the blessing
of Sufism and contentment.

Evil (*sharr*) and the Ultimate Evil (*sharr-i sharr*)

Author: Evil is your manifestation of existence, and the ultimate evil is that you are not aware that you have no existence of your own.

***

Abū Saʿīd b. Abī l-Khayr: Evil is you, and the ultimate evil is you without your knowing it. (AT 320)

The Law (*sharīʿat*), the Path (*ṭarīqat*) and Reality (*ḥaqīqat*)

Author: The law is the refining of the *nafs*; the Path is adornment of the heart with virtuous attributes; and Reality is renunciation of one's own existence and non-existence.

***

Shiblī: The law is worshipping God; the Path is seeking God; and Reality is seeing God. (TA 633)

Abū Bakr Wāsiṭī: The way of the adherents to the law is that of affirmation. If one denies one's existence under the law, one falls into heresy. However, in the way of Reality, if one affirms one's existence, one falls into unbelief. In the domain of the law affirmation is necessary, but in the domain of Reality negation is necessary. (TA 740)

With law as shell,

Reality is the kernel;
Between the two
lies the path.

Shabistarī

Kindness towards Others (*shafaqat bar khalq*)

Author: All are manifestations of God. If one loves God, one exercises kindness towards God's manifestations. Kindness to others means to see one's own comfort as dependent on other people feeling ease.

***

Abū l-Ḥasan Kharaqānī: The scholar rises at dawn to seek more knowledge; the ascetic seeks increase in asceticism; but Abū l-Ḥasan is committed to bringing joy to the heart of his brother. (TA 683)

Junayd: Kindness towards others means willingly tending to their every want and not imposing any burden on them which they cannot bear, nor telling them what they do not understand. (TA 448)

Abū ʿUthmān Ḥīrī (on being asked to what extent he practiced kindness towards others): To the point where I would be willing for God to subject me to all the torments in hell in place of those who have transgressed. (TA 393)

Bāyazīd: O Lord, at the Resurrection give me a role between Your decree and Your creatures. Let me shoulder their burden, for they are weak and have no endurance. (AAK 129)

Abū ʿAlī Siyāh: Nothing significant comes out of your happiness. The point is to make others happy. (KAM II 695)

Junayd (to a disciple): Do such as to make things easy for others and difficult for yourself. (KAM VII 475)

Sarī Saqaṭī: I desire that the sorrow which weighs on the hearts of others be upon my heart instead, so that they may be free of sorrow. (TA 331)

Thanks (*shukr*)

Author: Thanks is constantly recalling the grace and mercy of God shown towards you.

***

Abū ʿUthmān Maghribī: Thanks means awareness of your own helplessness in the fullness of gratitude for God's bounty. (TA 785)

Junayd: Thanks is the *nafs* not considering itself deserving of God's bounty. (TA 444)

Abū Bakr Warrāq: Thanks for God's bounty means seeing His kindness while observing its sanctity. (RQ 263)

Anonymous: The thankful one is one who gives thanks for what is at hand, while the most thankful one is one who gives thanks for what is lost. (RQ 264)

Recognition of the Divine Unity of Being (*shinākht-i tawḥīd-i wujūd*)

Author: Recognition of the Divine Unity of Being requires the non-being of the wayfarer.

***

Shiblī: Your gaining of gnosis of God by your own cognition, your perception of God by your own knowledge, your reasoning by your own understanding and imagination of God, and your control of things by your own ideas in your heart of God—these are all vain inventions that you make on your own and that refer back to you. (KAM III 438)

Wāsiṭī: There is no one to accept the recognition of the Divine Unity of Being, and there is no one having the gumption to set out into the desert of Being.

If one addresses one's own being through God's Being, one puts a stamp on one's unbelief. If one addresses God's Being through one's own being, one attests to one's dualism.

If one seeks one's being with His Being, one is an unbeliever. If one seeks His Being with one's own being, one is unaware.

If one is aware of oneself, one is not aware of God, for one can be aware of God only if one is not aware of oneself.

The soul went soaring in joy and came to rest behind the veil of the Grandeur. (TA 736)

Wāsiṭī: The Divine Light holds everything in Its bosom. It calls, "Come to the desert of Being, where the fire of jealousy-in-love (*ghayrat*) consumes everything." (TA 737)

Ad-Daqqāq: When a sufi was asked where God is, he replied, "May God banish you! How can you seek the 'where' of witnessing?" (RQ 21)

Muḥammad b. Wāsiʿ: I have never seen anything without seeing God therein. (TA 58)

When have You left my heart
that I should appeal to You?
When have You been hidden
that I should discover You?

You have not absented Yourself
that I should seek Your presence.
You have not manifested Yourself
that I should reveal You.

Furūghī Basṭāmī

Yearning (*shawq*)

Author: Yearning is the restlessness of the heart in seeking the Sought One.

***

Qushayrī: Yearning means the heart's rising to behold the Beloved. It is measured by the extent of the love within one. (RQ 575)

Abū ʿAlī Ad-Daqqāq: The difference between yearning and longing (*ishtiyāq*) is that the former ceases to exist while beholding, while the latter continues even while beholding. (RQ 575)

Naṣrābādī: All creatures are at the station of yearning, whereas no one is at that of longing. Whoever experiences the state of longing has reached the point where one has neither trace nor place. (RQ 575)

Ruwaym: Yearning comes when the traces of the Beloved cause you to lose stability and witnessing Him annihilates you. (TSS 184)

Lust (*shahwat*)

Author: A human being's wants are that person's lust.

***

Ibn ʿAṭāʾ: The heart enjoys lust of one kind, the spirit another, and the *nafs* yet another. That of the heart is witnessing, that of the spirit nearness to God, and that of the *nafs* pleasure in ease. (TA 492)

The Preacher (*wāʿiẓ*)

Author: When the term 'preacher' is used in Persian literature, it signifies one who is a sanctimonious advisor and does not practice what he preaches.

***

The preacher came criticizing me,
"Don't drink wine; it is illicit."
I said, "Fine, but I do not
pay much heed to any old ass.

The Master of the Winehouse narrates
beautiful tales, so

I'm sorry; I don't accept
the advice which you hand out."

Ḥāfiẓ

Our preacher has not had a whiff
of Truth —Be mindful of these words.
I would say this to his face;
I won't talk behind his back.

Ḥāfiẓ

Preachers say one thing
in mihrab *and pulpit;*
they do something else
when they're in private.

I have a problem to pose
to the scholar of the flock:
"Why do those who demand
repentance themselves repent less?"

It seems they do not believe
in the Day of Reckoning,
subjecting the work of the Judge
to corruption so perverse.

Ḥāfiẓ

I'm a disciple of the Master of the Winehouse;
don't be bothered by me, O preacher.
The fact is that you gave the promise,
but he gave it realization.

Ḥāfiẓ

Last night from the lane of the wineshop
they bore upon their shoulders
the city preacher who slung
his prayer-mat over his shoulder.

Ḥāfiẓ

Patience (*ṣabr*)

Author: Patience is seeing whatever comes your way as coming from God; and hence, accepting it with heart and soul, the good and bad of it being the same to you. Patience is also said to be the absence of restlessness in the face of undesirable events.

***

Abū Sulaymān Dārānī: I swear by God that not having patience with what we love, how can we be patient with what displeases us? (TbA 389)

Junayd: Patience means restraining the *nafs* while focusing on God without any sense of strain. (TA 445)

Junayd: Patience means swallowing the bitter without making a face. (TA 445)

ʿAmr b. ʿUthmān Makkī: Patience means standing with God and receiving affliction cheerfully and lightly. (TA 455)

Abū Saʿīd Kharrāz: Once out in the desert I was overcome by hunger, and the *nafs* craved something from God to eat. I said to myself that desiring something was not the work of those who trust in God. So I kept silent.

Disappointed, the *nafs* tried another trick. "Since you don't want anything to eat," it said, "then exercise patience for a while."

So I resolved to be patient. God had mercy on me. I heard a voice, saying, "This friend of Ours claims that We are close to him; and We are obliged not to let go to ruin such a person who approaches Us, seeking from Us food and patience, and who displays his abject helplessness and impotence, supposing that neither had he seen Us nor had We seen him."

ʿAṭṭār's commentary: This means that in seeking food, he had become veiled, seeking food from other than God. Likewise, in seeking patience, he was equally veiled, for patience is practiced with respect to what is other than God as well. (TA 458)

Ruwaym: Patience means abandoning complaint. (RQ 281)

Abū Muḥammad Jurayrī: Patience is that which does not distinguish between the state of bounty and that of trial, maintaining a calm *nafs* in the face of both. (TA 581)

Shiblī: The patient one is among those who stand in the antechamber [of God], while the contented one stands in God's presence. On the other hand, the one who is utterly consigned to God is one of God's intimates. (TA 633)

Sarī Saqaṭī was asked about patience, and as he was about to elaborate on its meaning, a scorpion fell on his foot and stung him several times while he stood still. When asked why he had not shaken off the creature, he replied, "I was ashamed before God not to practice patience when I was about to sermonize about it." (RQ 285)

When a man approached Shiblī, testing him to state what form of patience was most difficult to practice, the master replied, "Patience before God." When the man said it was not this, Shiblī said, "Patience for the sake of God." The man said it was not this either. "Patience with God," said the master. When the man said this too was not the case, Shiblī then asked what it was. "Patience from God," replied the man. Shiblī let out a cry, wanting to give up his life then and there. (RQ 281)

Anonymous: Perseverance is the ultimate patience, to the point where patience becomes drowned in patience and patience becomes disabled by patience. (RQ 283)

Association (*ṣuḥbat*)

Author: In our time it is better to renounce association with others. However when associating with others it is better to observe the following points of conduct:

1. With your elders, behaving with service; with those younger than yourself, with kindness and compassion; and with your contemporaries, with consideration (giving them priority) and chivalry.
2. Overlooking peoples' faults and not looking down on them.
3. Not harming or harrassing others.
4. Not gossiping about others.
5. Giving good advice to others, but opposing your own *nafs*.
6. Trying not to impose your own ideas on others.
7. Not speaking loudly in the presence of masters and elders.
8. Observing etiquette both outwardly and inwardly.

***

Qushayrī: Association is of three kinds:

1. With companions who are better than you; this is actually service.
2. With one who is less fortunate than you; this involves charity and loving-kindness. Fidelity and respect are necessary in this relationship.
3. With your equals and peers, a relationship characterized by chivalry and the favoring of others over yourself. (RQ 502)

Anṣārī: It is not correct to keep the company of strangers. First know them, then keep their company. (TSA 107)

Abū Bakr Warrāq: Do not associate with those who praise you for what you are not or what is not in you, because whenever they become angry with you for what they fail to find in you, they will start condemning you. (TA 375)

Veracity (*ṣidq*)

Author: Veracity obtains when the tongue is in tune with the heart.

***

Junayd: The reality of veracity is speaking the truth in a crisis from which you could be saved only by lying. (TA 444)

Dīnawarī: Only veracity can take a human to the ranks of the most virtuous ones. To lack sincerity at any time or in any state makes that time and state valueless. (TSS 478)

Yūsuf b. Isbāṭ: A night spent working veraciously with God is dearer to me than wielding a sword in the way of God. (TA 503)

Nahrajūrī: Veracity is conformity with God both inwardly and outwardly. The reality of veracity is to speak truthfully even under threat of destruction. (TSS 378)

Anonymous: Veracity is one's inner being being in harmony with one's speech. (RQ 328)

When you seek veracity
from knowledge, you win;
When in your approach you try
to be clever, you die.

Sanā'ī

The *Ṣirāṭ* Bridge (*ṣirāṭ*)

Author: You must pass over the *Ṣirāṭ* Bridge of your existence to reach the heaven of Unity.

***

Kharaqānī: When you have gone beyond your existence, you have crossed the *Ṣirāṭ* Bridge. (AAK 55)

Devotional Practice (*ṭā'at*)

Author: Devotional practice is to follow God's command and to serve Him without anticipating or even paying attention to a reward.

***

Ḥuṣrī: In daily prayers, try to be unaware of the prayers, and in fasting, try to be unconscious of the fasting. Devotional practice is a formality. The reality is to be effaced therefrom.

Rūzbihān's commentary: This means that if you seek the reality of devotional practice, be unconscious of your worship of the Eternal Creator, so as not to be veiled from the Worshipped One by your very practice, for the reality of worship is to be effaced in the consciousness of God from consciousness of the practice. If you want to be liberated from your self, set the pearl of mystery rolling on your tongue, with the double purpose of letting God communicate His message to Himself through you and of rushing you on without delay, spurring the steed of pre-eternity. As soon as you are aware of Him, you leap from the sound and fury of the tumult to be liberated from the pitfalls in the garden of daily prayers. (SS 589)

Junayd: Devotional practice is not a cause for what has occurred in pre-eternity; rather it indicates that what the devotee has done has been virtuous. (TA 437)

Abū Bakr Wāsiṭī: I have no interest in a God who is satisfied with my devotional practice and is angry with my transgressions. Such a God is in bondage to me, as he awaits what I would do. No, the fact is that the true friends are the pre-eternal ones, and the true enemies likewise. (TA 744)

Wāsiṭī: Avoid the pleasures of devotional practice, for they generate poisons. (TSA 226)

Wāsiṭī: When one has the reward for devotional practice before one's eyes, seeking merit, one forgets God's grace. (TSA 226)

Shiblī: Ordinary people occupy themselves in their affairs, while the worshippers of God engage in devotional practice and canonical commandments. One who is occupied with one's affairs is obsessed with fear of being incapacitated, while one who is engaged in devotional practice and canonical commandments is afraid of being disgraced. (HyA X 368)

Devotional practice is not
just planting one's brow on the ground.

Bring forward sincerity,
for it's not on the forehead.

Saʿdī

Drink wine, for a hundred
sins veiled from others
are better than sanctimonious
devotional practice done for showing-off.

Ḥāfiẓ

Seeking the Way (*ṭalab-i ṭarīq*) and Seeking God (*ṭalab-i Ḥaqq*)

Abū Saʿīd b. Aʿrābī: One who seeks the Way commits himself to going towards God by means of the Way with the utmost of spiritual striving, whereas one who seeks God directly proceeds without need of the Way and its guides, where God is his guide to Himself, bringing him into Union precisely. (TSS 430)

Seeking (*ṭalab*), Finding (*yāft*) and Witnessing (*mushāhada*)

Author: Seeking, finding and witnessing all represent

success and favor granted by God.

***

Kharaqānī: In all matters, seeking comes first, then finding, except on the sufi Path, where finding comes first, then seeking.

He also said: There are those who give indications of finding without knowing that finding is impossible; and there are those who give indications of witnessing without knowing that witnessing is a veil. (TA 698)

ʿAlī b. Sahl Iṣfahānī (when asked to discuss finding): The closer one thinks one is to God the farther one actually is. When the sun shines through a window, children reach out to seize the particles. Thinking that they have them in hand, they open their fists to find nothing there. (TA 543)

Abū Saʿīd b. Abī l-Khayr: The moment you think you have found God is the very moment you have lost Him. (AT 276)

Junayd: Witnessing is the maintenance of Lordship and the disappearance of devoteeship, on the condition that you do not remain in between.

He also said: Witnessing means going into direct vision of something without being conscious of the essence thereof. (TA 443)

Anṣārī: The pleasure is in the seeking, not in the finding.

Finding is a blow which knocks you down. (TSA 149)

I will not give up seeking
until I am fulfilled;
Either my body reaches the Beloved
or my soul leaves my body.

Ḥāfiẓ

Greed (*ṭamaʿ*)

Author: Greed is the attribute of one who seeks more than God has apportioned to him.

***

Muḥammad b. ʿUmar Warrāq: If they ask greed who its father is, it replies, "Doubt in the face of what is apportioned." If they ask what its occupation is, it says, "Baseness." If they ask its ultimate goal, it answers, "Utter deprivation." (RQ 62)

The Gnostic (*ʿārif*)

Author: The gnostic is one who experiences his own

existence as being annihilated in Absolute Existence.

***

Abū ʿAlī Ad-Daqqāq: The only knowledge which the scholar is qualified to give is that which can be read, whereas the knowledge which the gnostic gives is that which is experienced. (TA 656)

Nassāj: The first veils of the gnostic are knowledge, intellect and retreat. Until these three are lifted, the horse of one's aspiration will not spring into action on the battlefield of seeking. (TH II 563)

Imām Ja'far Ṣādiq: The believer is one who stands with his *nafs*, whereas the gnostic is the one who stands with his God. (TA 17)

Sarī Saqaṭī: The beginning of gnosis is detachment of the *nafs* from the world, for the sake of asserting God's singularity. (TSA 97)

Sarī Saqaṭī: The gnostic has the attribute of the sun radiating throughout the whole world, and the form of the earth, which bears the burden of all existents. He is, in essence, water, which is the foundation on which the life of hearts is based, and he is in color like fire, which brightens the world. (TA 339)

Bāyazīd: The source of the gnostic's inspiration is never darkened, such that whatever impurity comes to it becomes purified. (TA 194)

Bāyazīd: The devotional practice of gnostics is guarding their breaths for God's sake, because they have abandoned everything on encountering Him. (NKAT 101)

Abū Saʿīd b. Abī l-Khayr: Before becoming a gnostic, one seeks help from all quarters. Once one has attained gnosis, through God one becomes free of everything; indeed, all things are in need of Him. (TA 462)

Abū Muḥammad Murtaʿish: The gnostic is the prey of God, Who hunts him in order to elevate him and Who honors him by seating him in His sanctuary. (TA 517)

Nahrajūrī: The gnostic who has the greatest gnosis of God is the one who is the most confounded in God. (TA 508)

Shiblī (when asked what is meant by one's being a gnostic in Witnessing God): This occurs when the Object of Witnessing is manifest, the signs of witnessing are annihilated, and the senses disappear. (LT 36)

Muẓaffar Qaramīsīnī: The heart of the gnostic is for his Lord, and the body of the gnostic is for His creation. (TSS 396)

Dhū n-Nūn: The more one is a gnostic of God the more intensely one becomes bewildered by God because the closer one gets to the sun the more confounded one becomes, until one reaches the point where one no longer exists. (TA 151)

ʿAlī b. Sahl Iṣfahānī: The rational live according to God's decree; those who remember God live through God's mercy; and the gnostics live through nearness to God. (TA 544)

Jaʿfar Khuldī: The gnostics are those who are not themselves. If they are themselves, they are not themselves. (TSA 496)

Abū l-ʿAbbās Qaṣṣāb Āmulī: If you are conscious of God, you cannot say, "I am conscious of Him." (TA 643)

Abū Bakr Wāsiṭī: There are four things which are not appropriate or worthy for the gnostic: asceticism, patience, trust-in-God, and contentment, for these four things are attributes of form, whereas the spirit is beyond them. (TA 741)

Bāyazīd: Ordinary people have states, while the gnostic does not, for the gnostic's characteristics are effaced and his being is annihilated in the Being of Another, with any trace of the characteristics of the gnostic disappearing in those of the Other One. (RQ 543)

Dīnawarī: The ascetic becomes exhausted in his body, and the gnostic exhausted in his heart. (TSS 516)

Junayd: The gnostic is one about whose inner being God speaks, while the gnostic remains silent. (RQ 548)

Abū Turāb Nakhshābī: The gnostic is one who is darkened by nothing and in whom all dark things are purified. (RQ 549)

Shiblī: The disciple speaks, while the gnostic remains silent. (TSA 64)

Abū Sulaymān Dārānī: The gnostic is the one, while lying in bed, to whom are revealed secrets which are never revealed to the one who stands in daily prayers. (TA 282)

Rābiʿa: The gnostic is the one who wants a heart from God. When God gives him one, he immediately returns it to Him, so that he may remain safe in His grip and in His secret (*sirr*), being veiled from phenomenal beings. (TA 81)

Abū l-Qāsim Muqrī: The gnostic is one whom God keeps preoccupied so that he does not think about accepting or rejecting others. (TSS 512)

Dhū n-Nūn: The gnostic seeks self-sufficiency from God. When one becomes free of need through God, becoming constantly in remembrance of God and with God keeping him in the bosom of His mercy, God makes him intimate with Him. (KAd 255)

Worship (*ʿibādat*) and the Worshipper (*ʿābid*)

Author: True worship is the manifestation of non-existence in the presence of God.

***

Yaḥyā b. Muʿādh: To me the merest particle from the Beloved is worth more than seventy years of worship without love. (TA 370)

Abū Ḥafṣ Ḥaddād: Outward worship seems like celebration but is really pride, because it is a matter of overreaching what is apportioned. The principle is that one can never be made joyful by one's own acts, only prideful. (TA 399)

Abū Bakr Wāsiṭī: One who worships God for heaven is no more than a mercenary of his own *nafs*. One who worships God for God's sake is also ignorant, because God has no need of one's worship. Do you think that you are doing anything for His benefit? You are only serving yourself! (TA 743)

Kharaqānī: Daily prayers and fasting are the work of worshippers, whereas removal of blight from the heart is the work of true human beings. (AAK 121)

Bāyazīd: God is aware of the hearts of His friends. When He sees that certain of them cannot bear the burden of gnosis of Him, He occupies them with worship of Him. (TA 193)

Seclusion (*ʿuzlat*)

Author: Seclusion is stepping away from what is other than God.

***

Ibn ʿAṭāʾ (on being told by a man that he wanted to go into seclusion): When you go away from people, what are you going to attach yourself to?
The man: So what should I do?
The master: Be outwardly with others and inwardly with God. (TA 495)

Love (*ʿishq*)

Author: Love is the Divine attraction which takes the sufi from his self, so that everything becomes Him.

***

Abū Naṣr Sarrāj: Love is the fire which blazes in the breasts and hearts of lovers, burning to ashes everything other than God. (TA 640)

Kharaqānī: When I asked myself if there were a more yearning devotee than myself, God opened my inward eye so that I might see His yearning devotees. I was ashamed at my unworthiness. I wanted to show others too the love of the chivalrous so that they might know that not every love is real love, and then they would be ashamed to say to their beloved, "I love you." (TA 685)

Kharaqānī: When one falls in love, one finds God. When one finds God, one forgets oneself. (TA 709)

Abū Saʿīd b. Abī l-Khayr: Love is the trap of God. (TA 324)

Bāyazīd: When one is slain by God's loving-kindness, the blood-money God gives is vision of Him. When one is slain by God's love, the blood-money God gives is to sit with Him. (AM 56)

Kharaqānī: Love is a benefit from the Sea which phenomenal beings cannot cross. It is a fire which the soul cannot pass through. The devotee has no awareness of its coming and going. (TA 708)

The physician of love is the Jesus-breath
which heals you.
Only One Who sees pain in you
can treat you.

Ḥāfiẓ

Human and jinn are parasites
on the being of love
Maintain devotion, that you may
gain felicity.

Ḥāfiẓ

I practice loving in the hope
that this noble art
won't become a disappointment
like the other crafts.

Ḥāfiẓ

Love is a flame
which, when it spreads,
leaves all but the Beloved
completely consumed.

Mathnawī

Love can't be contained in
what's spoken or heard;
Love is a sea
whose depths can't be seen.

Mathnawī

God's Bestowal (*ʿaṭā-yi khudāwand*)

Author: God's bestowal is given without invoking obligation to Him. Any sense of obligation comes from the devotee. To the sufi, bestowal and trial are the same, because both are considered to have come from God, and whatever comes from God is good.

***

Abū l-ʿAbbās Sayyārī: Bestowal is of two kinds: bestowal out of munificence and bestowal intended as incitement to advancement. If it is meant for you to gain something, this is out of munificence, whereas if you lose something thereby, it is intended to incite you to advance [on the Path]. (TA 779)

Intellect (*ʿaql*) and the Reasoner (*ʿāqil*)

Author: The intellect is the doorkeeper of the heart, while love is the king of the heart.

***

Abū Ḥafṣ Ḥaddād (when asked who the reasoner is): One who seeks release from the *nafs*. (TA 398)

Abū l-Ḥusayn Nūrī (on being asked the proof of God's existence) : God.

He also said (when asked the state of the

intellect): The intellect is impotent, and the impotent can prove only what is impotent like itself. (TA 473)

Bāyazīd: Reason is sufficient for the believer to understand that God has no need of one's actions. (NKAT 105)

Ibn ʿAṭāʾ: The intellect is the tool of devoteeship, not the surveyor of Lordship. (TA 494)

Wāsiṭī: When God appears, reason is set aside. As God comes closer to the devotee reason runs away because it is helpless. It is even too helpless to realize that it is helpless. It is in the nullification of reason that God's intimates have gnosis of Lordship, because reason is the means of maintaining devoteeship, not the means of experiencing the reality of Lordship. (TA 741)

Reasoners are the point
of the compass of existence, but
Love knows that they are
confounded in this circle.

Ḥāfiẓ

Reason and Love (*ʿaql wa ʿishq*)

Author: Love is the work of the heart and is God's attractive force. Reason is born of the brain and is led astray by worldly knowledge.

***

The following are a few verses on reason and love:

O reason, begone!
There's no place here for the rational.
If you were hair-thin,
not a hair of you would fit here.

Day broke, and every lamp
which claimed to bring
daylight was put to shame
by the flames of the sun.

Rūmī

On the way of seeking,
rational and mad are one;
in the school of love the stranger
and one's kin are one.

When one is given
the wine of Union with the Beloved,
in His religion the Kaʿba
and the idol-temple are one.

Rūmī

In the session of lovers
there is another dispensation,
where this wine of love
gives a different headiness.

The knowledge that one
has learned in school
works differently from
the way love works.

Rūmī

Love circulated like
the blood flowing in my veins,
till it utterly emptied me
and filled me with the Friend.

All the limbs and organs
of my being took on the Friend;
Of me there is only a name;
the rest is all the Friend.

Rūmī

Reason came,
and set about advising the lovers.
It sat upon the Way and
started highway robbery.

Since in their heads
advice failed to take hold,
reason kissed their feet
and went upon its way.

Rūmī

Fire burned up the being of
a hundred rational ascetics;
this is the burning
which we set on our crazy hearts.

Ḥāfiẓ

Love is a stranger to
both of the two worlds;
within it are seventy-two
forms of craziness.

It is deeply hidden,
but the bewilderment it causes is visible;
The souls of kings are driven
to agonized sighing over it.

Its faith is apart from the classical
seventy-two religions;
the thrones of monarchs are so much
lumber compared with it.

The minstrel of love strikes up

this refrain in time of audition:
"Let devoteeship now begin
and Lordship be broken up."

So what then is love?
The sea of non-existence.
There the eternal
destroys intellect.

Mathnawī

Love should be pursued
so one flies to the very heavens.
Reason should be pursued,
so that one learns knowledge and conduct.

Rūmī

Particularizing reason
is the denier of love,
even if it appears
To be the possessor of mysteries.

Mathnawī

The lover's sickness
is different from other sicknesses;
love is the astrolabe
of the mysteries of God.

However I try to explain
the meaning of love,
when I come to love itself,
I'm ashamed thereof.

As the pen rushed
to write it out,
on reaching 'love',
it split apart.

Trying to chart it, reason was
like a donkey stuck in the mud;
only love itself was equipped
to express love and loving.

Mathnawī

Love is a master at whose
hand I have drunk the cup.
Reason is a child who has
become learned in our school.

Furūghī Basṭāmī

Let the ascetic who has not become
spiritually shrewd be forgiven;
love is work which is attuned
to inward spiritual guidance.

Ḥāfiẓ

The heart is a burning candle lit by the Beloved,
a cleft of separation stitched together by the Beloved.
O you who are unaware of inner burning:
Love must arrive; it cannot be taught.

Rūmī

I bound my head with strict commitment
to mosque and prostration;
I donned the badge of asceticism
to do more good deeds.

Love came into the mosque and cried,
"O reverend master, rip off
the bonds of existence!
Why be attached to the prayer-hall?

Don't let the heart shake in fear
before the thrust of my sword.
Offer your neck if you want to travel
from knowledge to vision.

Rūmī

Love is no more than
fortune and grace;
It's no more than guidance.
and opening the heart.

Abū Ḥanīfa

did not rule on love;
Shāfiʿī has given
no transmitted report of it.

Permitting and forbidding
obtain till death;
the knowledge that is for lovers
has no end.

Rūmī

Reason, too, is love and not
foreign to the savor of vision.
But reason, poor wretch, is not bold enough
to have spiritual shrewdness.

Iqbāl Lāhūrī

One may see the face of the Unseen
Beloved with the eye of love,
for the light of the lover's eye
shines from one peak of Mt. Qāf to another.

Ḥafiẓ

An instructive verse about love
came from the ledger of reason;

I fear you don't really know
what truly is known by this lesson.

Ḥafiẓ

I appealed to precedent and ruled
with reason on love,
like writing on the surface of the sea
with drops of dew.

Ḥāfiẓ

To speak about love
with reason is
like sticking a lancet
in a dead vein.

Ṣā'ib-i Tabrīzī

In pre-eternity a ray of Your Beauty
shone forth in theophany;
Love appeared, and all the world
was engulfed in flames.

Love sought to light a lamp
with those flames.
The lightning of God's jealousy flashed
and caused uproar in the world.

A claimant sought to come
and view the mystery;
a hand from the Unseen
struck the unwelcome breast.

Ḥāfiẓ

Reprisal (*ʿuqūbat*)

Author: Reprisal for the sufi comes in paying attention to what is other than God.

***

Abū Bakr Kattānī: Being attached to what is created brings reprisal; being close to the worldly is transgression; and inclination towards any of them is degradation. (TA 568)

It is justice that you acquit us
with reprieve from reprisal;
it is grace that you draw the line
of pardon over our error.

Ḥāfiẓ

Knowledge (*'ilm*) and the Knower (*'ālim*)

Author: From the sufi point of view the only knowledge is that of loving.

***

Junayd: The knowledge of God's Unity comes from God's Being, while His Being is distinct from knowledge of Him. (TA 442)

Kharaqānī: There is exoteric knowledge, ultra-exoteric knowledge, esoteric knowledge and ultra-esoteric knowledge. The exoteric knowledge and ultra-exoteric knowledge are what the clerics profess, while the esoteric knowledge is what the chivalrous profess. The ultra-esoteric knowledge is the secret communication which the chivalrous have with God and to which the ordinary have no access. (TA 695)

Nūrī: God is the only guide to God. Now the purpose of knowledge is service.

Hujwirī's commentary: This means that you should use your cognition for the purpose of serving, not to sharpen cognition itself. (KM 345)

Bāyazīd: Knowledge is treachery, gnosis trickery, and witnessing veiling. So how are you going to find what you seek? (TA 196)

Ibrāhīm Adham: Along the way, I came across a stone on

which was inscribed: "Turn me over and read me." So I turned it over, and there was written: "You who do not put your knowledge into practice, how can you seek what you do not know?" (KM 12)

Muḥammad b. Faḍl Balkhī: Knowledge (*ʿilm*) has three letters: *ʿayn*, *lām*, *mīm*. *ʿAyn* stands for *ʿilm* ('knowledge') itself, *lām* for *ʿamal* ('practice'), and *mīm* for one who is *mukhliṣ* ('sincere') in knowledge and practice. (TA 519)

Muḥammad b. Faḍl: The knower's error is more harmful than the ignorant person's deliberate intention. (TSS 215)

Abū Bakr Kattānī: Knowledge of God is more perfect than worship of God. (TA 568)

Aḥmad Anṭākī: The director of all actions is knowledge, and the director of all knowledge is favor. (TA 412)

Abū Saʿīd Kharrāz: God has made knowledge the guide to Himself, that He might be known; and He has made wisdom a mercy from Himself upon those who seek Him, that they might gain familiarity with Him.

To be exact, knowledge is the guide towards God and gnosis the guide to Him. So through the knowledge you may gain information [about Him], while through gnosis you may reach God Himself. Knowledge is achieved through learning, and gnosis through direct experience. Gnosis comes about through the process of coming to know God, while knowledge brings perception in the knowing of phenomenal beings. The attainments of each flow forth in a way appropriate to each. (TSS 230)

Abū ʿAlī Thaqafī: Knowledge is the life of the heart, freeing it from ignorance, and the light of the eye, freeing it from the darkness of ignorance. (TSS 364)

Abū Bakr Ṭamastānī: Knowledge separates you from ignorance. Now try not to let it separate you from God. (TSS 474)

Junayd: Knowledge is knowing your own worth. (TA 442)

Junayd: What casts the knowers away from God's eye is something like the greed for the kind of knowledge which is not established in their hearts. (HyA X 263)

Ḥārith Muḥāsibī: One who is a knower through the motions of the heart at the site of the Unseen is better than one who is a doer through the motions of the limbs. (KM 134)

Shāh Shujāʿ Kirmāni: One who is ignorant dwells in the darkness of his own ignorance, but the fact is that when one who knows falls into the darkness of his own knowledge, the darkness of knowledge is harsher. (TSS 194)

Abū Bakr Warrāq: People are of three kinds: the

scholars, the paupers, and the leaders. When the scholars go wrong, their followers go wrong. When the paupers go wrong, their morality goes wrong. When the leaders become corrupt, the people's sustenance becomes corrupt. (KM 179)

Abū Bakr Warrāq: The knower is less than what he says. The sage is on a par with the words he says. The realized gnostic is higher than what he says. (TSA 317)

Who told you
to flip from page to page?
Turn the page
and behold the Truth.

Raḍiy ad-Dīn Ārtīmānī

The fields of knowledge are porters
for the people of heart,
but they are no more than burdens
for the bodily folk.

When knowledge hits the heart,
it provides aid;
when it hits the body,
it becomes a load.

There is no real knowledge
but that of loving.

The rest is the deceit
of wicked Satan.

Mathnawī

Wāsiṭī: Gnosis is bearing witness through the senses directly, while knowledge is through information. (TSA 649)

Rote knowledge is the curse
of our souls;
it is something borrowed, while
we sit on wealth.

Though it serves to carry
your reason on high,
your rote-learning bird
feeds down below.

Mathnawī

How distasteful is
rote knowledge,
learned like something
which is overheard!

It is looking for grain,
not for enlightenment;

and so it is base like
the seeker of worldly knowledge.

The seeker of knowledge
wants what's general or special,
with no interest in finding
liberation from this world.

Mathnawī

Rote knowledge is for selling;
when it finds
a customer, it has
traded well.

Mathnawī

Abū ʿAlī Thaqafī: The fullness of knowledge is the severance from hope of reaching the essence of the matter. (TSS 363)

Nahrajūrī: The best thing one can do is to commit oneself to knowledge. (RQ 75)

Abū Saʿīd Aʿrābī: The paths of knowledge lead to intermediations, while the paths of realities lead to revelations. (TSS 430)

Festival (*ʿīd*)

Author: Festival for the sufi means severance from self and becoming God's sacrifice, that is, returning to the Origin of the Unity of Being.

***

There's no New Year's Day nor festival
to celebrate for Your Majdhūb;
he will celebrate festival on that day
when he becomes a sacrifice for you.

Majdhūb Tabrīzī

The Vision of Certitude (*ʿayn al-yaqīn*), the Knowledge of Certitude (*ʿilm al-yaqīn*) and the Truth of Certitude (*ḥaqq al-yaqīn*)

Author: The meaning of the vision, knowledge and truth of certitude is that one sees, knows and comes to know Reality with certitude.

***

Muḥammad b. Faḍl Balkhī (on being asked how one can attain soundness within): By being constant in expectation of the truth of certitude. This is the life which leads to the knowledge of certitude being granted, leading to the contemplation of the vision of certitude, whereby soundness comes about. The vision of certitude must precede the knowledge of certitude. If one has not seen the *Kaʿba*, one can never enjoy the knowledge of certitude of the *Kaʿba*.

Thus, it is clear that the knowledge of certitude must come after the vision of certitude. Whatever knowledge precedes vision is that which is based on aspiration (*himmat*) and spiritual striving, and that is why it is sometimes right and sometimes wrong. Once the knowledge of certitude appears, one may contemplate the mysteries of the truths of the vision of certitude. By way of example, if one were to fall into a well and grow up there, then suddenly be pulled out, one would become confounded in the sunlight, staying in this state for a while, until one's constitution adjusted to the sunlight. The objective is that one gain from the sunlight the knowledge to contemplate the mysteries of the sun. (TA 518)

Alienation (*ghurbat*)

Author: The sufi is in alienation in this world and the next.

***

Abū Ḥamza Khurāsānī: Alienation is the sufi's becoming adverse to his relatives and those to whom he is connected, becoming a stranger to them. (TA 552)

Kharaqānī: The alienated one is not merely one whose body is alienated in the world, but one whose heart is alienated in his body and whose inner consciousness is alienated in his heart. (AAK 110)

I'm an alien in this town,
a pauper in this realm;
I'm caught in your lasso,
a captive in your trap.

Saʿdī

Overwhelmings (*ghalabāt*)

Author: Overwhelmings represent the loss of consciousness of self when the devotee becomes overwhelmed by theophany of the Lordship.

***

Rūzbihān: Overwhelmings represent the soaring of the spirit in the angelic realm (*malakūt*), the gliding of the inner consciousness (*sirr*) in the realm of power (*jabarūt*), the onrush of attraction in theophany of the Divinity, and the pre-eternal essence (*huwiyat*) shaking spirits and bodies. (SS 553)

Gossip (*ghaybat*)

Author: When one gossips about someone else, one is simply ascribing one's own flaws to someone else.

***

When Ḥasan Baṣrī was told that a certain man was gossiping about him, he sent him a tray of halvah with the message: I heard that you were sending all your attributes to me as a gift, so I wanted to give you something in return. (RQ 236)

Junayd: I was sitting in the Shūniziyya Mosque, along with a crowd of Baghdadians, awaiting the arrival of a corpse, so that we could observe the prayers for the dead. I saw a dervish with the signs of devotional practice upon him, yet he was begging from the people. I thought to myself, "If you're a proper dervish, you would have a decent job to look after yourself."

When I got back home, I could not concentrate on my nightly litanies. My regular prayers and other devotional practice were a real struggle for me, with much weeping on my part. Then I could not get to sleep for a while, worrying about my litanies. Then I suddenly fell asleep. I dreamt of that dervish being brought to me as a meal on a platter.

"Eat of his flesh," I was commanded. "After all, you were gossiping about him." [Reference is to Koran 49: 12.] God had found me out.

I protested that I had not gossiped about him; I

had only thought something to myself.

"You are not one of the ordinary," came the answer. "that God should be content with you behaving like them. You have to seek His forgiveness."

When day broke, I set out to find the dervish, looking here and there. Finally, after a long search I found him sitting by a stream, rinsing off blades of chives which had floated downstream. I greeted him, and he said, "Do you still reject the message of that occurrence?"

"No," I replied. "May God have mercy on us both." (RQ 237)

Jealousy-in-Love (*ghayrat*)

Author: For the sufis jealousy-in-love has two aspects: that of the lover and that of the Beloved. The latter is where God wants the lover strictly for Himself, while the former is where the sufi does not disclose to anyone his secret with God.

***

One school of thought among the sufis: Jealousy-in-love is an attribute of the novice, whereas the adherent to Divine Unity is not aware of anything other (*ghayr*) than God at all. Such a one has no volition, not seeking to control events in the world about him and seeing God as higher than anything else he might want. Jealousy-in-love is of two kinds: that of God towards the devotee, which prevents the devotee from being distracted by others by stealing him away from them; and that of the devotee towards God, which keeps his states and moments from involvement with anything other than God. (RQ 421)

Once Shiblī gave the call to prayer, but when he opened his mouth to bear witness to the Prophet's apostleship, he stopped short, saying, "Had it not been your order to do so, I was not going to mention anyone else with You." (RQ 425)

Maghribī: Jealousy-in-love is an attribute of disciples, not of the adepts. (TA 785)

Shiblī: Jealousy-in-love is twofold: the human kind, which affects bodies, and the Divine kind, which affects hearts. When the latter touches breaths, it becomes corrupted through anything other than God. (RQ 421)

Jealousy-in-love cuts out
the tongues of the elect.
Since when was the secret of yearning
for Him expressed by the common?

Ḥāfiẓ

Heart-discernment (*firāsat*)

Author: Heart-discernment is to know others without

asking questions.

***

Abū Bakr Wāsiṭī: Heart-discernment is an illumination glowing in hearts and a gnosis emerging in the inner consciousness, carrying the devotee from one perception of the Unseen to another, till he sees things which God manifests to him, informing him about the core of other people's nature. (RQ 367)

Qushayrī: Heart discernment is a thought that comes into a person's heart and removes everything there that opposes it; thus, it rules the heart. (RQ 366)

Ḥallāj: When God overwhelms the innermost heart, it becomes the possessor of secrets, sees them and tells others about them. (RQ 366)

Abū ʿUthmān Ḥīrī: Heart-discernment may be correct or in error unless one has become realized, in which case insight becomes realized in its judgment because in this condition it judges by the light of God, not its own. (TSS 174)

When Abū Isḥāq Kāzirūnī finished addressing one of his meetings, a scholar present suddenly rose and went over and kissed his hands and feet. "What's this all about?" asked the master.

"When you were speaking," replied the scholar, "it occurred to me that my knowledge is greater than yours. I thought, 'While I struggle to make a living and earn a crust of bread for myself, this master is welcome everywhere and has riches showered upon him. What is the wisdom in this?'

"No sooner had this flashed in my mind than you fixed your eye on this lamp and said, 'The water and the oil in this lamp were boasting to one another.

"'"I am more precious and learned than you," said the water, "for your life and that of everything else depends on me. So why are you sitting above me?"

"'"Because," replied the oil, "I have suffered much, going through a reaping and a pounding and a pressing which you haven't seen. And after all this, I burn and burn to give people light, while you just go your own way. Yet if anyone throws anything on you, you hiss and boil and raise a fuss. That's why I stand above you."'" (TA 766)

Abū Jaʿfar Ḥaddād: Heart-discernment is what comes to you without opposition. If there is opposition, then it is merely the talk of the *nafs.* (RQ 372)

Singularity (*fardāniyyat*)

Author: Singularity refers to the Oneness and Uniqueness of God. In the station of singularity, the sufi melts in the Oneness of God.

***

Rūzbihān: In singularity, knowledge, understanding, description and the desire to articulate, all become annihilated. Then the Singular and One remains in His Singularity beyond the vicissitudes of temporality, createdness, knowledge, understanding and time. (SS 541)

Obligatory Practice (*farīḍa*) and Customary Practice (*sunnat*)

Author: Obligatory practice means abandoning self-consciousness, while customary practice means abandoning the world and the hereafter.

***

Bayazīd: Obligatory practice means associating with God, and customary practice means abandoning the world. (TbA 399)

Poverty (*faqr*) and the Pauper (*faqīr*)

Author: Poverty means having need for nothing other than God.

***

When Bāyazīd was asked if poverty could be described,

he replied, "Of course! Owning nothing and being owned by nothing." (TbA 399)

Junayd: Poverty is the heart's being empty of forms. (TA 445)

Yaḥyā b. Muʿādh Rāzī: The reality of poverty is that it will never be satisfied except through God. The procedure of it is that one not be conscious of any secondary cause. (RQ 453)

Munāzil: The reality of poverty is severance from the world and the hereafter and finding sufficiency in the God of this world and the hereafter. (TA 541)

When Ibn Jalāʾ was asked when the devotee becomes worthy of poverty, he explained, "Whenever poverty is credited to the dervish and he also claims it, this is not poverty, because it involves consciousness of the *nafs*. Whenever poverty ceases to be claimed and the *nafs* is not involved, then true poverty obtains, and the one who enjoys it is a true dervish." (RQ 457)

Sufi saying: The pauper is not one who has no worldly goods; the pauper is one whose very nature is free of desire. (KM 28)

Muḥammad b. Manṣūr Ṭūsī: The reality of poverty is calmness in the face of any lack, and generosity towards every being. (TSA 126)

Junayd (on being asked whether poverty or wealth is better): Virtue lies in piety, not in poverty or wealth. (TSA 188)

Once when Abū Saʿīd b. Abī l-Khayr went to the public bath in Nishapur, the eminent jurisprudent, Abū Muḥammad Juwaynī, came to see him at his *khānaqāh*. On being told that the master had gone to the bath, Juwaynī went off himself in hopes of catching him there. As he entered, the master asked him how he liked the bath.

"It's fine," replied Juwaynī.

"Why is it 'fine'?" countered the master.

"Because the master is here," answered the worthy jurisprudent.

"You can answer better than that," said the master.

"Please say it," urged Juwaynī.

"Because you have nothing but a loincloth and a bucket," answered the master, "and neither of them belongs to you either." (AT 227)

Abū Saʿīd b. Abī l-Khayr: Wealth is a hardship one cherishes, while poverty is a relief one does not cherish. (AT 303)

Annihilation and Subsistence (*fanā wa baqā*)

Author: Annihilation is the loss of self, while subsistence means joining in Divine Unity.

***

Abū Saʿīd Kharrāz: For the devotee, annihilation means the annihilation of the devotee, while subsistence means subsistence of the devotee in the Divine presence.

He also said: Annihilation means disappearing in God, while subsistence means being present with God. (TA 461)

Kharaqānī: When you see yourself with God, this is fidelity, while when you see God with yourself, that is annihilation. (TA 705)

Rābiʿa: O Children of Adam! There are no stages from the eye to God nor any access from the ear or tongue to Him. The highway is too much for talkers, while the hands and feet of human beings are confounded. The work therefore has fallen to the heart. Strive that you may gain an awakened heart, for when the heart awakens, it has no need for the Beloved.

ʿAṭṭār's commentary: This means that the awakened heart is one which is lost in God. If one is lost, what need does one have for the Beloved? This is annihilation in God. (TA 81)

Abū Saʿīd Kharrāz: The annihilated one is one whose pleasure in the world and the hereafter has vanished, so that only God remains. (TSA 181)

Ibrāhīm Shaybānī: The knowledge of annihilation and subsistence depends on sincere profession of God's oneness and upright devoteeship. Anything else throws you into error and drags you into heresy. (RQ 77)

Anonymous: Annihilation means becoming purified of blameworthy attributes, and subsistence means acquiring praiseworthy ones. Once one becomes characterized by one of these two states, one is always in one or the other. When one enters, the other goes away, each following the other. When one becomes annihilated from blameworthy characteristics, praiseworthy ones take over one. When one is overcome by blameworthy traits, one becomes stripped of praiseworthy ones.

Know that whatever may be ascribed to the devotee comprises actions, temperament and states. Actions are what the devotee controls by his own will, and temperament belongs to his material nature, though subject to curative treatment, given that it has become a matter of habit. The states enjoyed by the devotee come to him at first, but they may become purified by the devotee's actions.

Since temperament is of this nature, when one gains the traits of a good temperament, one naturally rejects those of a bad temperament by one's own efforts, seeking aid and success from God, that He might make one's temperament good. Correspondingly, when one takes care to purify one's acts by one's striving and persistence, God grants the grace of purifying one's states.

When one avoids blameworthy actions in terms of the religious law, one is said to have become annihilated from one's passions. Once one has done this with sincere resolve, one becomes subsistent in one's devoteeship.

When one renounces the world through one's heart, one is said to have become annihilated from desire. Once one has done this, one becomes subsistent in contrition (*inābat*).

When one subjects one's temperament to curative treatment, rooting envy, spite, meanness, anger and pride out of one's heart, with the actions relating to these being removed from the volatility of the *nafs*, one is said to have become annihilated from the bad traits of temperament. Once one has done this, one becomes subsistent in veracity and chivalry.

When one becomes conscious that control and dictates are under God's power, one has become annihilated from the process of time and from phenomenality. When one has become annihilated from attention to the works of phenomenal beings, becoming aware that one has nothing to do with them, one becomes subsistent in the Attributes of God.

When one is overcome by the domination of Reality to the point where one has no consciousness of anything other, neither essence nor effects, one is said to be annihilated from phenomenal being and to have become one with God. One's annihilation belongs to one's praiseworthy states, whereas one's blameworthy states obtain in the absence of such actions.

One's annihilation is from both one's *nafs* and

from phenomenal beings. It is such that one does not sense one's self and them. When one has become annihilated from states, actions and temperament, it is not right to say that they do not exist. Rather, one has become oblivious to one's *nafs* and to phenomenal beings, being conscious of neither.

When one becomes annihilated from one's ignorance, one becomes subsistent in God's Knowledge. When one becomes annihilated from the passions, one becomes subsistent in renunciation. When one becomes annihilated from craving, one becomes subsistent in renunciation. When one becomes annihilated from self-seeking, one becomes subsistent in devotion [to God].

All of one's attributes follow accordingly. When one becomes annihilated from one's own attributes, such that one has no consciousness whatsoever of them, one goes beyond this to become annihilated from the very consciousness of annihilation.

It has been said that the beginning of annihilation is from one's *nafs* and personal attributes to subsistence in God and His Attributes. Then annihilation from the passions means utter obliteration in God's Being. (RQ 106)

Contraction and Expansion (*qabḍ wa basṭ*)

Author: Contraction or sorrow means becoming absent

from self, and expansion or joy means becoming present in God.

***

Nūrī: Contraction gives you what is for yourself, whereas expansion gives what is for God. (MH 424)

Ahmad b. ʿAṭā, Rūdbārī (on being asked about the states and attributes of contraction and expansion): Contraction is the first of the causes of annihilation and expansion the beginning of those of subsistence. The state of someone in contraction is that of absence and that of one in expansion, presence. The attribute of someone in contraction is that of sorrow and of one in expansion, joy. (TSS 499)

Qushayrī: Contraction and expansion are the two states which come after one has experienced fear and hope. Contraction for the gnostic is what fear is for the beginner, while expansion is the stage of hope for the novice.

The difference between contraction and fear is that fear is of something which may happen, such as the loss of the Beloved or the sudden occurrence of a misfortune, whereas contraction is a spiritual reality (*maʿnā*) which is acquired in the moment.

The difference between expansion and hope is that hope is of something like the arrival of the Beloved or the relief of a misfortune or the acceptibility of something now disapproved of in the future, whereas expansion is a spiritual reality, like contraction.

One who experiences fear and hope connects his heart to what is yet to come, while one who experiences contraction and expansion is immersed in his moment and the infusion which overcomes him in the present state. Thus, the realities of the two pairs are different by their very nature, where the devotee has no control over contraction and expansion.

Both states come as the result of an infusion (*wārid*). In the case of contraction, an infusion may cause the contracted one to experience things as he would normally, or an infusion may result in one not being affected at all by what occurs around him, because he has transcended all this.

In the case of expansion, the expanded one may have one of two effects: either he may have an expansion where he experiences the impact of phenomenal beings but does not become upset by them in most cases, or he may remain unaffected by any of them in whatever state. (RQ 94)

Contentment-with-Sufficiency (*qanāʿat*)

Author: Contentment-with-sufficiency means dealing with what is at hand and not needing what one does not have.

***

Ibn Khafīf: Contentment-with-sufficiency means not

seeking what you do not have in hand and having no need of what you do have in hand. (TA 578)

When Bāyazīd was asked how he had arrived at where he was, he replied, "I gathered up all the things of the world and tied them up with the rope of contentment-with-sufficiency and put them in the catapult of sincerity and hurled them into the sea of despair and found relief." (RQ 243)

Qushayrī: When during the Pilgrimage season a crowd of Iranian disciples were seated around their master Junayd, a man came in with five hundred dinars, which he placed in front of the master, saying that it was to be distributed among the assemblage.

"Is this all you have?" asked Junayd.

"I have much more," the man replied.

Junayd asked, "Do you need any more wealth?"

"Yes," the man answered.

Junayd then told him to pick up what he had deposited there and keep it, saying, "You need this gold more than anyone else." The man refused to accept it. (RQ 243)

Anonymous: The good life is contentment-with-sufficiency in this world. (RQ 239)

Bishr Ḥāfī: Contentment-with-sufficiency is a monarch who is at peace only in the heart of the believer. (RQ 239)

Another master: Contentment-with-sufficiency means acquiescing to what exists and not seeking more. (RQ 240)

Dhū n-Nūn: Whoever enjoys contentment-with-sufficiency is at ease with those around him, becoming greater than his contemporaries. Whoever chooses contentment-with-sufficiency becomes relieved of distraction in the heart, beoming nobler than his contemporaries. (RQ 241)

Cardinal Sins (*kabāʾir*)

Author: One of the biggest of the cardinal sins is to express one's own existence.

***

Abū Turāb Nakhshabī: God has told us to avoid committing cardinal sins. These can be summed up as making corrupt claims, pointing to what is false, and making ascriptions on the basis of empty statements and hollow expressions without truth. (TA 359)

Pride (*kibr*)

Author: Pride means being conscious of yourself and not of God.

***

Ḥātim Aṣamm: If one were to weigh the pride of the ascetics, clerics and Koran-reciters of our age, it would come out far heavier than that of the princes and kings. (TA 301)

Abū Hāshim Kūfī: It is far easier to dig up a mountain with a needle than to root pride out of one's heart. (TSA 7)

Livelihood (*kasb*)

Author: The sufi strives to work and earn a livelihood in society, believing that an idle person is a parasite on society, and a parasitic person cannot be a sufi.

***

In Junayd's teaching, earning a livelihood is not compulsory, but it is considered devotional practice. (KST 244)

ʿAbd Allāh Manāzil: Engagement in earning a livelihood is better than retreat without a livelihood. (TA 542)

The Sufis' Clothing (*libās-i ṣūfiyān*)

Author: Sufism does not mean wearing special clothes.

***

Kharaqānī: There are many wearers of sackcloth, but trueness of heart is what is required. What benefit is there in special dress? If wearing sackcloth and eating barley could make you an adept, many a donkey would be advanced on the Path! (TA 702)

Abū ʿAlī ad-Daqqāq: Wear what everyone else wears and eat what everyone else eats, but be apart from them in your inner consciousness. (RQ 155)

Abū ʿAbbās Dīnawarī: Outward dress will not change inward state. (TSS 477)

Luminous Manifestation (*lawāʾiḥ*), Effulgence (*lawāmiʿ*) and Auroral Illumination (*ṭawāliʿ*)

Qushayrī: Luminous manifestation, effulgence, and auroral illumination are terms which are close to one another, in fact, little different from one another. They are attributes of novices on the Path, having yet to become illuminated in heart by the light of the sun of gnosis.

Nonetheless, God is giving provision to their hearts at every moment. Whenever their hearts are darkened by the fog of sense-pleasures, the lightning of visionary revelation (*kashf*) flashes upon them and the effulgence of nearness shines forth, as they await luminous manifestaion in a time of shrouding (*sitr*).

Luminous manifestation comes first, then comes effulgence, and finally auroral illumination. Luminous manifestation is like a bolt of lightning which flashes, then disappears, leaving only an afterglow.

Effulgence is more apparent than luminous manifestation and does not disappear so quickly. It remains for two or three moments. When it shines forth, it cuts you off from yourself and gathers you to itself, although it has not yet become the full light of day to drive away the army of the night.

Auroral illumination lasts longer. Its domination is strong, sweeping away the darkness more effectively, as accusations (*tuhmat*) are chased farther away, though it is still in danger of declining and is still not lasting. One is fearful of its departure, though its fading is gradual.

As to the nature of the three states, they observe various processes. In some cases, when they go, they leave no trace, like the passing stars, such that when they disappear, it seems that night has truly fallen.

In other cases, traces are left, as when the moment of the state passes, but the pain of it remains, where though its light has faded, its traces stay. After the lingering of its domination, the one who experiences it comes to thrive in the light of its blessings until it returns another time. He lives in anticipation of its return, in the meantime comfortable with what he has. (RQ 119)

Loving-kindness (*maḥabbat*) and Friendship (*dūstī*)

Author: Loving-kindness is a gift from God; it cannot be earned or learned by the devotee.

***

Qushayrī: Loving-kindness for the devotee is a state from God which one receives in one's heart through grace. This state is indescribable; it makes the devotee reverent towards God, causing him to seek God's contentment, to be patient in the face of God's trials, to be joyful through God, to be uncomfortable with what is other than God, and to gain lasting intimacy with continual remembrance of God in his heart. (RQ 556)

Dhū n-Nūn: In the course of my travels I encountered a woman whom I asked, "What is the ultimate loving-kindness?"

"Silly idler," she replied, "loving-kindness has no ultimate degree."

When I asked why, she explained, "Because there is no ultimate degree to the Beloved." (TA 146)

When Rābiʿa was asked if she loved God and she said that she did, she was then asked if she considered Satan to be her enemy.

"My love for the Benevolent is such," she replied, "that I can't be involved in hostility with Satan. In fact, I dreamt that the Prophet asked me if I loved him.

"'Who doesn't love you?' I answered. 'But love for God has penetrated me so deeply that no love or enmity towards anything other than Him is left in my heart.'" (TA 80)

When a guest of Abraham sought to take leave of his host, he asked Abraham to point out his defects to him. "I've seen no defects in you," replied Abraham, "because I've looked at you through the eyes of loving friendship. As a result, whatever I saw from you I found pleasing." (TA 116)

Bāyazīd: The sign that one loves God is that one has three qualities: generosity as wide as the sea, kindness as warm as the sun, and humility as meek as the earth. (TA 193)

Maʿrūf Karkhī: Loving-kindness cannot be taught by human beings, for it is a gift and a grace from God. (TA 328)

Junayd: Friendship is not realized between two persons unless they can address each other, "O, I!" (TA 443)

Junayd: Friendship is where the attributes of the Beloved take the place of those of the lover. (TA 447)

Abū Saʿīd Kharrāz: When God wants to turn a devotee of His into a loving friend, He opens the door of remembrance for him. Then once the devotee gains pleasure in remembrance, God causes the door of chivalry to open for him. Thereupon he enters the house of the Singularity, and the site of the Majesty and the Grandeur is revealed to him. Then, whenever his eye falls upon God's Majesty and Grandeur, he becomes subsistent, and the essence of his being becomes preserved by God. (TA 460)

Abū ʿUthmān Ḥīrī: Loving-kindness that is worthy of its name is the effacement of everything but the Beloved in the heart. (TA 481)

Junayd: Loving-kindness is extreme longing. (RQ 563)

Samnūn Muḥibb: Loving-kindness is the fundamental principle of the Path. States and stations are all a game compared to loving-kindness. (TA 510)

Qushayrī: In the case of the devotee, God's loving-kindness is a blessing for him, where devotion is for the sake of bounty. Mercy is higher than devotion, and loving-kindness is higher than mercy. (RQ 554)

Kharaqānī: If You place me in the realm of loving-kindness, I would get drunk in love for You; whereas if You place me in the realm of awe, I would go mad due to Your sovereignty. (TA 687)

Sufi saying: Loving-kindness is an intoxication from which the devotee becomes sober only on beholding the Beloved. As for the intoxication which comes in the course of witnessing, it cannot be described. (RQ 567)

When Shiblī was confined in the Baghdad asylum, a group of sufis came to visit him. When he asked who they were, they replied that they were his friends. He began throwing stones at them, so they all ran away. Calling after them, Shiblī cried, "If you claim to be friends of mine, why can't you put up with my tormenting you?" (RQ 566)

When a certain man approached a youth on a rooftop, claiming to love him, the latter asked how this could be, declaring that he had a brother who was more handsome. When the man looked back to see the brother, the young man threw him off the roof, saying, "If someone claims to love me, and then looks at someone else, this is what he gets!" (RQ 569)

Abū Bakr b. Yazdānyār: True loving is complete agreement with something, and the lover is he who makes pleasing his beloved more important than anything else. (TSS 408)

Shiblī: When Majnūn was asked if he loved Laylī, he said, "No." When asked why, he said, "Loving is a means to union, and the means has fallen away. So Laylī is I, and I am Laylī." (TbK I 105)

Yaḥyā b. Muʿādh Rāzī: The reality of loving-kindness is that it is not increased by benefit nor lessened by betrayal. (KM 404)

Aḥmad b. ʿĀṣim Anṭākī: The sign of loving-kindness is that one says as little about it as possible, while reflection on it is lasting, involving much retreat, and silence about it is constant. When one looks upon loving-kindness, one does not see it. When one calls, it does not hear. When trouble strikes, it is not upset. When good fortune befalls it, it is not overjoyed. It fears no one and has no hope in anyone. (TA 410)

Samnūn Muḥibb: No description could be fine enough or subtle enought to define loving-kindness. In fact, it is beyond definition.

(When asked why loving-kindness is associated with calamities): So that not just any low-thinking person may claim it. When such a one sees calamity, he simply gives up. (TA 513)

Dhū n-Nūn: When God loves you, He keeps you enshrouded, having jealousy-in-love (*ghayrat*) about you. When you love Him, He makes you famous, calling people to you. (ST II 216)

Dhū n-Nūn: There is nothing dearer than God's loving, though it does not take hold in a heart in which there is love for anything other than God. (ST II 216)

Shiblī: Loving God is a form of consternation (*dahshat*)

in pleasure and a kind of bewilderment (*ḥayrat*) in reverence. (IU 625)

The Claimant (*muddaʿī*)

Author: Whoever claims to know God is a veiled false claimant.

***

Dhū n-nūn: Every claimant is veiled by his own claim from vision of God and from hearing God's word. If God is present to someone, such a one has no need to make claims, whereas if God is absent, his claim of knowing God exposes his veiledness. (TA 155)

Ibn ʿAṭā: The greatest of claims is when someone claims to know God and is constantly referring to God, or when someone speaks of God with ever greater exaggeration. These are all the qualities of liars. (TA 491)

Ibn ʿUliyān: Whoever shows off his miracles is a false claimant, whereas one through whom miracles are made manifest involuntarily is a friend of God (*walī*). (TSS 418)

Meditation (*murāqaba*) and Attention (*tawajjuh*)

Author: Meditation is the sufi's burning away of thought of everything but God, forgetting his very self, devoting himself completely to the Beloved. The difference between meditation and attention is that in a state of attention the sufi is conscious of self, making a conscious effort to engage with God, whereas in a state of meditation the sufi has shed consciousness of self.

***

Rūzbihān: Meditation is the turning of the spirit towards the fragrances of God. (SS 572)

Shiblī: Going over to visit Abū l-Ḥusayn Nūrī, I found him sitting in meditation such that not a hair on his body was stirring. I asked him how he had learned so fine a meditation. He replied, "I learned it from a cat poised by a mousehole. And it was far more still than I." (TA 471)

Ḥārith Muḥāsibī: Meditation is the knowledge of the heart in nearness to God. (TA 273)

Junayd: Meditation means frightening off regret for what is past.

(When asked the difference between meditation and shame): Meditation involves awaiting the Absent One, while shame involves modesty before the Present One. (TA 443)

Ibn ʿAṭāʾ (when asked the highest form of worship): Constant meditation on God. (TA 495)

Jaʿfar b. Nuṣayr: Meditation is watching over your inner consciousness by witnessing God at each moment. (RQ 292)

Qushayrī: Meditation is the devotee's knowledge of God's awareness of him. The effort to carry on this knowledge leads to meditation on God Himself, which is the basis of all things. In this case one must harmonize one's breaths with God. (RQ 289)

The Patched Cloak (*muraqqaʿ*) and the Water-skin (*rakwa*)

Author: The patched cloak was the ragged garment which was stitched up and worn to show that one is a dervish. Considered to be a form of showing off, the custom no longer exists.

The water-skin was a leather container carried by dervishes, who filled it with water to quench the thirst when they were traveling.

***

Wearing the patched cloak was a declaration of being a sufi. Whoever wishes to associate with sufis must belong to one of the following groups:

God endows the inner consciousness (*sirr*) of one group of sufis with inward purity, outward charisma, subtlety of nature, temperance of constitution, and rectitude of spirit, so that they may experience the nearness of the realized ones and the high station of the eminent. The novice joins them in hope of attaining that degree. The beginning of their path involves the unveiling of states, detachment from passions, and turning away from the *nafs*.

God gives another group the experience of soundness of body, chastity of heart, stability, and health of breast in their manifestations, with the aim of making novices seek their company.

As for members of the third group, when they are accepted by the first group, granting them respect, they put on the woolen (*ṣūf*) garment, so that they may hide their blemishes under the guise of probity. When they don their garments, these clothes blatantly shout out their falseness. In our time members of this group are more numerous. If you invite them to accept the true Path, they will not agree to your Path for one instant, for the work of this Path has nothing to do with cloaks. When one comes to know this Path, all clothing is the same to one. When one is alien, one's very patched cloak shows the patches of rejection, actually publicizing one's wickedness. (KM 51)

Abū l-Qāsim Sīrwānī: I heard Abū l-Khayr Tīnātī say, "I was appointed to oversee hell. I noticed that the majority of the denizens were carriers of the water-skin and wearers of the patched cloak."

Sīrwānī's commentary: This would not be the actual case, and they would not be deserving of such a fate if they only had a little certitude. (TSA 569)

Humanity (*muruwwat*)

Author: Humanity is putting the rights of others before your own.

***

Ibn ʿAṭāʾ: Humanity is not making an issue of your actions for the sake of God. (TSS 267)

Abū l-Ḥusayn Būshanjī: Humanity is virtue of inner consciousness (*sirr*) and cheerfulness of countenance. (TSS 460)

Būshanjī: Humanity is not touching what is forbidden you. (RQ 80)

Naṣrābādī: Humanity is a branch of chivalry (*futuwwat*). It represents turning one's back on the two worlds and whatever is in them, feeling ashamed of them. (RQ 357)

The Disciple (*murīd*) and the Master (*murād*)

Author: The disciple is one who commits himself to the way of non-existence, while the master is he who does not exist. The disiciple should not object to the master in his heart, lest he fall off the Path.

***

Junayd: The disciple is burdened with knowledge and action, while the master is preserved by God, for the disciple runs along the ground, while the master flies. How could a runner ever compete with a flier? (TA 449)

Dhū n-Nūn: No disciple ever obeys God as well as his master does. (TA 155)

Junayd: Most of the obstacles which impede the disciple on the Path stem from the corruption of his original intentions. (AM 196)

Bāyazīd: For whomever has no master, Satan is his master. (AM 40)

Bāyazīd: When the disciple shouts and screams he is a mere pond, but when he remains silent he becomes an ocean full of pearls. (TA 196)

Abū ʿAlī Rūdbārī: The disciple is one who wants nothing

for himself unless God wants it for him, while the master is one who wants nothing from the two worlds but God. (KM 198)

Ḥallāj: The disciple is the one who aims at God from the very beginning, being at ease with nothing and engaged with no one until he attains God. (TSA 385)

Dhū n-Nūn: The disciple seeks with a hundred thousand pleas (*niyāz*), while the master, as the one sought, backs off with a hundred thousand airs (*nāz*). (TSA 22)

Muslim-ness (*musalmānī*) and the Muslim (*musalmān*)

Author: Muslim-ness means being with God outwardly and inwardly.

***

When Ḥasan of Baṣra was asked what Muslim-ness meant and who was a Muslim, he said, "Muslim-ness is in books, and the Muslims are all buried under the ground." (TA 33)

Witnessing (*mushāhada*), Visionary Revelation (*mukāshafa*) and Presential Vision (*muḥāḍara*)

Author: Presential vision is presence of heart with the aid of reason. Knowledge guides the heart in visionary revelation. Gnosis helps the heart in witnessing.

***

Abū ʿAlī Rūdbārī: Witnessing is for hearts, visionary revelation for the inner consciousness (*sirr*), direct vision (*muʿāyana*) for the inward eye, and spiritual practice for the outward eye. (TSS 358)

Qushayrī: Presential vision is in the beginning, followed by visionary revelation; then comes witnessing.

Presential vision is the coming of the heart into presence, due to a succession of proofs, although it is still behind the veil. Though one may be present, it is due to one's being overcome by the domination of the remembrance (*dhikr*).

After this comes visionary revelation, which involves one's coming into presence through clear evidence. One need not seek the proof or even seek a path. One is not beset by expressions of doubt, while at the same time one is not kept in the realm of the Unseen.

Next comes witnessing, which means being in the presence of God, where no doubt remains. This occurs when the heavens of the inner consciousness become cleared of the fog which blocks the sun of revelatory vision (*shuhūd*) shining forth from the constellation of noble overseeing. God witnesses this, as when Junayd said, "The existence of God appears when you lose yours."

Thus, the one who experiences presential vision is limited to the signs he observes. The one who is subject to visionary revelation rejoices in His attributes. The one who undergoes witnessing has arrived at Being, where doubt has no access.

The one who enjoys presential vision is guided by reason. The one who has visionary revelation approaches through his actions. The one who experiences witnessing is effaced by his gnosis.

No one could add to what ʿAmr b. ʿUthmān Makkī said about the realization of witnessing, when he stated, "It is where the light of the successive theophanies of God shine upon one's heart without anything obstructing it or cutting it off. It is like a dark night illuminated by an uninterrupted stream of light which never flags or slackens. The situation is such that the night is actually brightened into day. The heart is thus, being completely turned to day under continuous theophany, with night being utterly dispersed.

Nūrī said, "Witnessing is not realized by the devotee if a single vein amongst all the members of the body remains apparent."

He also said that when the sun comes out, there is no need for a lamp. (RQ 117)

The Polytheist (*mushrik*)

Author: As long as you are you, you are a polytheist.

***

Bāyazīd: For forty years I was the watchman of my heart. After forty years I came to see it as a polytheist. Its polytheism lay in the corner of its eye being aware of what is other than God. (TA 168)

When a disciple asked Junayd, "O you
Who know all of the mysteries inside out,
Reveal to me who is the polytheist?"
He said, "Babble is stupid, and he who
Uses God's name and has not seen Him yet
Is the crude meddler and the polytheist.
He who said, 'I am the Truth', but not through God,
Is counted also as an infidel.
Deniers of God as well are polytheists,
Making me, like their God, despair of them!
When dualism is raised from in between,
You won't remain, which He shall testify."
One Friday, Shiblī went up to the pulpit
In order to deliver that week's sermon.
He started off discussing God's pure oneness:
"He's only one, though there be thousands there."
Junayd who happened to be present said,
"O you who've sacrificed your very soul,
The things that I confided once in you

Why now divulge so openly to others!"
Shiblī said, "Peerless master of our time,
Put aside polytheistic talk right now!
I keep on speaking and I keep on listening,
For there is none but 'I' in the two realms!"

Dīwān ʿAṭṭār

Gnosis (*maʿrifat-i Ḥaqq*)

Author: Gnosis means acknowledging one's inability to know God.

***

When Bāyazīd was asked when one could expect truly to have gnosis of God, he explained, "When one becomes annihilated while being conscious of God and subsistent in God's space without ego-identity or individual humanity. One becomes alternately annihilated and subsistent and back again. One is a dead person come alive, and a living person who dies, a veiled person become unveiled, and an unveiled one covered again." (TA 199)

Qaṣṣāb: If one were to seek a god other than God, one would be a dualist. One should seek God as God, find God as God, and know God as God. (TA 643)

Ibn Yazdānyār: Gnosis means the heart's realization of

God's Oneness. (TSS 409)

Junayd: Gnosis is God's deception. This means that if one thinks he is a gnostic, he is deceived. (TA 442)

Dhū n-Nūn: Reflecting on God's Essence is ignorance, and pointing to Him is polytheism. The reality of gnosis is bewilderment (*ḥayrat*). (TSA 330)

Junayd: Gnosis is the existence of your inability to know at the moment when you receive knowledge about yourself. When asked to elaborate, he said, "the gnostic and the Known One are both He." (TA 442)

Shiblī: Gnosis is a bird in a cage. No matter where it sticks its head out, it cannot escape. (TA 633)

Shiblī: The beginning of gnosis is God; it has no end. (RQ 542)

Qushayrī: According to the sufis, gnosis forces one to become absent from one's *nafs* through one's being dominated by remembrance of Him, so that one sees nothing but God and refers to nothing else. The fact of the matter is that whereas the intellectual refers back to his heart and his reflection, when a problem arises for the gnostic, he refers directly to God.

The gnostic refers only to his God. One cannot refer to one's heart if one has no heart. There is, furthermore, a difference between one who lives in one's heart and one who lives through one's God alone.

(RQ 542)

Wāsiṭī: Gnosis is twofold: the special and the established.

The first is shared, being a polytheistic gnosis of the Names and Attributes, the guidelines, the signs, the proofs, and the veils.

The second is one to which there is no access. It arises from the Eternal, and when it appears your own gnosis becomes insignficant, dwindling to nothing because your gnosis is transitory, so that when the mode of the Eternal appears in theophany all transitory things are obliterated. (TA 742)

Bāyazīd: Whoever points to Him through knowledge is preaching unbelief, since pointing through knowledge can only be done to something knowable. Whoever points to Him through gnosis is limiting Him, because pointing through gnosis is only possible to limited things. (LT 224)

Shiblī: The reality of gnosis is the inability of gnosis. (KM 354)

Shiblī: When one knows God, one does not experience sorrow. (TSS 343)

Ḥallāj: Gnosis means seeing all things as obliterated in reality. (TA 588)

Abū l-ʿAbbās Sayyārī: The reality of gnosis is to go

beyond knowledge. (TSS 444)

Nūrī: Those who enjoy gnosis know a little about a little, because they know the proof or the way, but God is beyond this. (AT 260)

Sahl b. ʿAbd Allāh Tustarī: The end of gnosis is bewilderment (*ḥayrat*). (TSA 635)

Transgression (*maʿṣiyat*)

Author: The sufi's transgression is attention to what is other than God.

***

Tirmidhī: When one embarks on the Path, he has no quarrel with those who transgress. (TA 532)

When one becomes afflicted
with the Beloved,
One is liberated
from heart, faith, being and non-being.

Sabzawārī

Deception (*makr*)

Author: Deception is that which makes you conscious of yourself and keeps you from awareness of God.

***

Junayd: For the disciple, lack of awareness of deception is a cardinal sin, while for one in Union, it is unbelief. (TA 446)

Incurring Blame (*malāmat*)

Author: Certain masters have taken the way of incurring blame. The followers of God are noted for incurring blame from others. They have chosen this approach in order to avoid arrogance and pride.

***

When Bāyazīd approached home after going on the Pilgrimage, the news spread and the people flocked out to welcome him to escort him into the town. When he became involved with people, he lost track of God, becoming distracted. When he reached the marketplace, he took a crust of bread from his sleeve and began to eat it. The crowd backed off and left him alone, for this was during the month of Ramaḍān.

It was Ḥamdūn Qaṣṣār who made the way of incurring blame popular. He said, "Incurring blame means giving up one's well-being."

The more one abandons one's well-being and prepares to take on trials, forsaking all that is familiar and comfortable, cutting off expectation of others in the hope of unveiling the Divine Majesty, and not seeking worldly things in rejecting people, severing one's material nature from intimacy with them, the more one becomes disassociated from them and the more attached one becomes to God. (KM 72)

How can you reach the circle
of the clean-losing sharpsters,
If you do not smash your pitcher
with the stone of incurring blame?

Furūghī Basṭāmī

'I and You' (*'man wa tu'*)

Author: When one speaks in terms of self, such as by saying 'I and You', one is afflicted with one's *nafs*. Sufis say "The only veil between the sufi and God is the self."

***

Kharaqānī: O Lord! Do not keep me at a station where I speak in terms of God and creation, or in terms of 'I and You'. Keep me at a station where I do not get in the way, where all is 'You'. (TA 688)

Kharaqānī: O Lord! I have been doing whatever pertained to me in Your name, and whatever pertained to You also in Your name, till the obstruction of 'I' is removed and everything is 'You'. (TA 688)

Kharaqānī: People believe that they may take something there [to the hereafter] which is appropriate for there. Nothing can be taken from here, let alone be taken there, except something which is strange for there, and that is non-existence. (TA 699)

Abū Saʿīd b. Abī l-Khayr (to a dervish complaining how a journey had exhausted and aggravated him): This is nothing. You set out on this journey for your own purposes. If you did not exist on this journey, if you had abandoned yourself even for a moment, you would have found peace yourself and others would have found peace in your company. One's prison is oneself. As soon as you step out of the prison, you find ease. (AT 222)

Abū Saʿīd b. Abī l-Khayr: It is easier to pull a mountain with a hair than to pull yourself out of your self. (AT 319)

Invited to a funeral ceremony, Abū Saʿīd arrived to be greeted by the ushers, who asked him how he should be introduced. Since most of the guests had titles, the ushers wanted to know how the master should be presented. He told them, "Go in and announce, 'Make way for Nobody son of Nobody!'" The ushers did as they were bid. When they made their announcement, the great and the good all heard and raised their heads to see who was coming. When they saw the master, they all fell into a state and wept. (AT 278)

Abū ʿAmr Zajjājī: If the being of my human nature could in any way be lessened, I would prefer that to walking on water. (NfU 222)

Qaṣṣāb: As long as 'I and You' remain, it is a matter of intimation and declaration. When 'I and You' are removed, neither intimation nor declaration is left. (TA 643)

When Qaṣṣāb was approached in Ṭabaristān, each person had a question or a request.

"O Lord!" Qaṣṣāb cried. "Each person must have something, and I must have nothing. Everyone must have a desire, and I must have none. Let it be that I must not exist." (AT 207)

Abū Bakr Nassāj: As long as you exist, what you imagine will never be burned away. The eye of the heart will not be stitched shut with the needle of jealousy-in-love (*ghayrat*) to what is other (*ghayr*) than God. The retreat-house of the soul will not be illuminated with the candle of theophanies from the Beloved, because the seed is not sown in the earth and the pattern is not inscribed on the decorated manuscript. (NfU 370)

Wāsiṭī: I and He! He and I! My doing and His rewarding! My prayer and His response! This is all dualism. (TSA 432)

Who are we in a world
all twisted up?
We're like a zero,
meaning nothing.

You are First and Last,
we are in between;
we are nothing at all
that can be expressed.

Mathnawī

My turban, my shirt and my head—
all three together
do not amount to as much
as a single dirham.

You have never heard
my name in the world;
I am nobody, nobody,
nobody I am.

Rūmī

Whoever knocks
at the ego's door
is turned away,
having knocked on nought.

Mathnawī

This ego is the ladder
of phenomenal being;
whoever climbs this ladder
will only tumble off.

The higher one ascends,
the more stupid one is,
for the bones of such a one
will more likely break.

Mathnawī

Harmony (*muwāfaqat*)

Author: Sufis are outwardly alive with the living and dead with the dead. They have no conflict with any group, faith or religion, looking upon everyone with the eye of loving-kindness, for they consider phenomenal being to be the manifestation of the Divine Being. This is why harmony on the Path is one of the principles of conduct on the Way.

***

O King of the lovers, have you ever seen
anyone more harmonious than I?
I'm alive with the living
and dead with the dead.

Rūmī

The Self (*nafs*)

Author: Whatever passes through the consciousness other than God is an occurrence of the *nafs*. The *nafs* is the core of selfishness, and one who is conscious of self will never be conscious of God.

***

Ibn ʿAṭāʾ (on being asked what the greatest enemy is with respect to God): Paying attention to the *nafs* and its states with expectation of reward for one's actions. (TA 492)

Anonymous: Don't put your reins in the hands of the passions, for they will pull you into the dark. (RQ 229)

Sahl b. ʿAbd Allāh Tustarī: There is no worship of God like opposing the passions and the *nafs*. (RQ 227)

Ibn ʿAṭāʾ: The constitution of the *nafs* is based on misconduct, whereas the devotee is enjoined to good conduct. The *nafs* goes forth into the arena of opposition [to God's way] as it has been constituted to do, while the devotee attempts to refrain from misbehavior by struggling against it. Whoever lets the *nafs* go unbridled will become its partner in corruption. (TA 492)

Abū Bakr Ṣaydalānī: Life comes only with the death of the *nafs*. The life of the heart depends on the death of the *nafs*.

He also said: One cannot emerge from the *nafs* through the *nafs*, but one can emerge from the *nafs* through God, though this can never happen without true devotion to God.

And he also said: The greatest blessing is to emerge from the *nafs*, because the *nafs* is the greatest veil between you and God. One can arrive at Reality only with the death of the *nafs*. (TA 721)

Abū Muḥammad Murtaʿish (on being told of a man who could walk on water): The one to whom God grants success in opposing the compulsions of the *nafs* is greater than one who can walk on water or levitate. (TA 516)

Abū Bakr Warrāq: The fundamental effect of domination by the *nafs* is its encouragement of lust. When desire dominates one, the heart becomes darkened; and when the heart is darkened, one sees others as one's enemy; and when that happens, others consider one their enemy. Then one begins to betray others and to oppress them.

He also said: Whoever falls in love with the *nafs* will become loved by pride, envy, depravity and corruption. (TA 536)

Abū Bakr Ṭamistānī: The *nafs* is like fire. Whenever you put it out in one place, it flares up somewhere else. In the same way, as soon as the *nafs* calms down in one area, it rears up in revolt in another. (TSS 474)

ʿAbd Allāh Manāzil: When one lifts the shadow of the *nafs* from within, others come to live in one's shade. (TSS 367)

Qushayrī: Literally, *nafs* means the existence of something. As far as the sufis are concerned, *nafs* in the absolute sense is designated as neither existence nor form, but rather the deficiencies of one's own attributes and one's blameworthy actions and temperament.

Two characteristics of the *nafs* stand out: first, its commission of wrongs like transgressions and opposition [to God's will]; and second, the base inherent character traits which are condemnable.

When one treats one's *nafs* as one would a sickness, and devotes oneself to spiritual striving (*mujāhadat*), the base and blameworthy traits of temperament go away with persistent effort.

The first issue is anything forbidden or declared dubious. The second issue is that of the bad traits of temperament, in summary, all flawed characteristics. These may be detailed as pride, anger, envy, spite, bad temper, lack of tolerance, and other bad characteristics.

The toughest problem of the *nafs* is that it imagines it is worthy and deserving of respect. This is considered to be a form of hidden polytheism. The improvement of one's character traits lies in forsaking and breaking the *nafs* as thoroughly as possible by starvation and deprivation of drink, along with wakefulness and other methods of spiritual striving which reduce the strength of the *nafs*. All of this constitutes forsaking of the *nafs*.

However, the word *nafs* may also mean a subtle

substance placed in the body, which is the repository of blameworthy character traits, in the same way as the spirit is a subtle substance in the body which is the repository of praiseworthy character traits. All of these parts are related to each other, and the combination froms a human being.

The *nafs* and the spirit are among the subtle bodies in the corporeal form, like angels and jinns in terms of subtlety. Just as it is evident that the eye is the site of seeing, the ear that of hearing, the nose that of smelling, the mouth that of tasting, where sight, audition, savor, smell, and savor all make up the human being, so similarly the site of blameworthy traits is the *nafs*, which, like the heart, is a constituent of this whole, and its role and name are related to the whole. (RQ 132)

The Cure of the *Nafs*

Among the eminent of Basṭām, there was an ascetic, a practitioner of rigorous austerity, who was known to frequent Bāyazīd's circle as well.

Once he addressed the master, "O Master, for thirty years I've been fasting and keeping the nightly vigil and have gotten nothing out of the science you teach, though I affirm and like it."

"Even if you fast and pray for three hundred years," replied the master, "you won't gain an iota of this matter."

When the ascetic asked why, the master said, "Because you are veiled by your *nafs*."

When asked what the cure is, the master replied, "In my view, there is a cure, but you won't accept it."

"I will accept it," the ascetic insisted. "I've been seeking it for years."

"Go rightaway," said the master, "and shave off your hair and whiskers, take off the cloak you are wearing and put on a rough loin cloth, then sit in the neighborhood where you are best known. Fill a bag with walnuts and put it in front of you. Call the children around you and tell them you'll give them a walnut for every slap they give you, two for two, and so forth. Then get up and go around the town, getting childen to slap you, for this is the treatment for your sickness."

"There is no god but God!" the ascetic shouted in protest.

The master answered, "If you were an unbeliever, saying these words would make you a believer, but with these words you became a dualist."

When the ascetic asked why, the master said, "When you said these two expressions, you were glorifying yourself, not God."

"I can't do what you told me," said the ascetic. "Tell me to do something else."

"Your treatment is this," said the master. "I warned you that you wouldn't do it." (TA 173)

Daily Prayers (*namāz*) and Fasting (*rūza*)

Author: Daily prayers and fasting put people on the course of God's favor and attention. The result is soundness of body and mind.

***

Junayd: If in the course of a round of prayers thought of the world passed my mind, I would do that set of prayers over again. If thought of the hereafter passed my mind, I would do an extra prostration to compensate. (SkS 171)

Bāyazīd (to a man doing prayers in a mosque): If you think that by doing your prayers you will reach God, you are wrong. This is all fantasy, not attainment. If you do not do your prayers, you are an unbeliever, and if you look at them for an instant and count on them, you are a polytheist. (TA 181)

Ḥallāj: Fasting is absence from seeing what is other than God for the sake of seeing God Himself. (TAQ 91)

Kharaqānī: Some of Your devotees like daily prayers and fasting, while others have a special fondness for the Pilgrimage or going on crusades. Still others have a particular feeling for theology and extra prayers. Make me one of those whose life and love is consecrated to You alone. (TA 689)

Muẓaffar Qaramsīnī: Fasting is of three types: that of the spirit, restraining expectation; that of the intellect, opposing desire; and that of the *nafs*, abstaining from food and transgressions. (RQ 75)

Abū Saᶜīd b. Abī l-Khayr: Shaikh Abū l-ᶜAbbās [Qaṣṣāb] often said, "If a disciple performs a single sufi service, this is better than a hundred extra rounds of daily prayers; and if a disciple eats a bite less, this is better than doing prostrations of prayers all night." (AT 264)

Kharaqānī: One who does the daily prayers and fasts will be close to people, while one who meditates will be close to God. (TA 708)

Once when Abū l-ᶜAbbās Qaṣṣāb was sitting in retreat, he heard the muezzin cry, "Let the prayers begin!"

"How hard it is," he exclaimed, "to come out of the center in the presence of God!"

Then he got up and went off to the congregational prayers. (TA 645)

To do prayers in the bend
of those mihrāb*-eyebrows*
one has first to purify oneself
with the blood of heartache.

Ḥāfiẓ

O coyly strutting quail,
with your jaunty gait,
don't be deceived by the pious cat
having just completed his prayers.

Ḥāfiẓ

If you don't do your prayers drunkenly,
though in the mosque, you are still engaging
in idolatry.

Ārtīmānī

Need (*niyāz*) and Freedom from Need (*bī-niyāzī*)

Author: As long as you are in the bonds of self, you are needy; when you lose your self you become free from need.

***

Abū Saʿīd b. Abī l-Khayr: Neediness is necessary. The shortest way to God is utter need. If neediness enters solid granite a spring will gush forth. The granite stands for the sufis, and the spring is the work of God's mercy. (AT 264)

Shiblī: My point of support is helplessness, and my cane is need for God. (TA 619)

Abū Ḥāzim Makkī: When one is content with God, one has no need for creation. (TA 67)

When the mighty Sultan Maḥmūd of Ghazna came to call on Abū l-Ḥasan Kharaqānī in his remote village retreat, he pitched his tent outside the master's hermitage and sent a messenger to summon him, telling the courier that if the master refused to come, the courier should recite the following Koranic verse: "They obey God and they obey the Prophet and the commanders amongst them" (4:59). When the messenger did accordingly, the master replied, "Tell Maḥmūd that I am so immersed in 'They obey God' that I fear that I will fall short in 'they obey the Prophet', let alone 'the commanders'."

When the messenger relayed this to the sultan, the latter was impressed and decided to go seek out the master himself, saying, "He is very different from what I thought." He decided to test the master by changing clothes with his retainer, Ayyāz, whom he decked out with all the royal weaponry and regalia. Then they set out with a small retinue to visit the master, who was not fooled for a moment by the change of dress. Completely ignoring Ayyāz attired as a king, the master remained seated but gestured Maḥmūd over, taking him by the hand from his sitting position and pulled him down next to him.

When the sultan called for him to speak, the master said, "First, send away those who are not privy." At Maḥmūd's behest the entourage all went trooping out. Then the visitor asked the master to tell him about Bāyazīd. So the master recounted that Bāyazīd said, "Whoever sees me is spared from damnation."

"This is beyond even the competence of the Prophet," exclaimed Maḥmūd, "for the likes of Abū Jahl and Abū Lahab and other deniers saw him, and they are among the damned!"

"Keep a civil tongue in your head!" admonished

the master. “Keep to your own field of competence! Only the Prophet’s Companions actually saw him. According to the Koran: ‘You see them looking at you, but they see not.’” (7: 198)

Delighted with these words, Maḥmūd asked for counsel.

“I’ll say this prayer on your behalf,” said the master: “O Lord, forgive the believing men and women.”

When Maḥmūd asked for a prayer specially for him, the master said, “May Maḥmūd enjoy a praiseworthy (*maḥmūd*) outcome!”

The sultan placed a purse of gold before the master, who in turn put a piece of barley bread before him, telling him, “Eat!” Maḥmūd gobbled it up, till it stuck in his throat.

“Don’t tell me it’s caught in your throat!” said the master. When the sultan replied that it had, the master said, “Do you want me to have that purse of gold stick in my throat? Take it away, for I have divorced the likes of it three times, once and for all.

When the sultan begged him to request something, anything, the master refused. whereupon the sultan asked for something personal from the master as a keepsake. The master took the aromatic shirt off his back and gave it to the sultan, who exclaimed, “What a fine hermitage this is!”

“So, with all that you have, you must have my hermitage, as well?” countered the master.

When Maḥmūd rose to leave, the master got up with him. Astonished, the sultan exclaimed, “When I first arrived, you did not bother about me. Now that I am leaving, you rise to see me off. What has prompted this sudden politeness? And what was the other treatment all about?"

"When you entered," said the master, "You were full of the pomp of royalty and the arrogance of testing me. In the end you depart humbled and as a sufi, with the sun of the fortune of Sufism shining on you. In the beginning I did not rise for your kingship. Now I stand up for your sufiness." (TA 668)

The Intermediary (*wāsiṭa*)

Author: The intermediary is said to be someone who puts himself between people and God, either to give guidance or to veil people.

***

Rūzbihān: The beneficence of the Eternal in maintaining humankind preserves people from extinction through intermediaries.

I do not prefer my wetnurse to my mother;
I am Moses; my wetnurse is my mother.

I do not want the grace of God by intermediary,
For this relationship has caused destruction of a people.

Mathnawī

The One Who Has Reached Union (*wāṣil*)

Author: When one becomes free from oneself one comes into Union with the Beloved.

***

Ibn Khafīf: The one-in-Union is one who is united with the Beloved, with nothing left but Him. (TSS 466)

Bāyazīd: I came into Union with Him only when I became detached from my self. Then again, I did not become detached from my self until I came into Union with Him. (TSA 171)

Being (*wujūd*) and Nothingness (*ʿadam*)

Author: God is Absolute Being, and what is other than God is nothingness.

***

Abū Saʿīd b. Abī l-Khayr (commenting on the Prophetic

Tradition: "One who knows one's self knows one's Lord."): One who knows one's self as nothingness knows one's Lord as Being. (AT 319)

Oneness (*Waḥdāniyyat*)

Author: Whatever is said about Oneness still falls short of defining it since the temporal cannot know the Eternal.

***

Ḥallāj: I consider You as being beyond the approach of Your slaves; through You, I have become weary of the Oneness which they witness in You. (SS 410)

The eloquent tongue is mute concerning Oneness. His Essence cannot be contained in the vessels of temporal things because these have bodily characteristics. Temporal things that are witnessed cannot represent Him. (SS 537)

Divine Unity (*tawḥīd*) is in essence Oneness (*waḥdāniyyat*), and Oneness has been the same before the world existed and will be the same after it ceases to exist. Emptiness and fullness become unknown and effaced next to unity. (SS 409)

Litany (*wird*)

Author: Litanies are expressions of being before God and smell of polytheism.

***

Abū ʿAlī Kātib: People who say litanies lack mystic hearts. (TSA 453)

Abū l-Ḥasan Sīrwānī: Sufis are devoted to God, not to litanies. (TSA 567)

Litany on the Tongue (*wird-i zabān*) and Remembrance in the Soul (*dhikr-i jān*)

Shiblī once said, "Allāh!" to Junayd.

"Is what you are saying," asked the latter, "a litany on the tongue or remembrance (*dhikr*) in the soul? If it is the former, remember that your tongue is secondary to your soul. If the latter, your soul should be detached from your tongue. Saying this is easy, because Iblīs says exactly what you are saying. Are you any higher than him? Do you have any special virtue? This is the domain of the ordinary. Both friend and foe come to it, both acquaintance and stranger. You have to be a serious devotee to attain the domain of the monarchs behind the veil. Otherwise, anyone, any piece of straw, can arrive at the domain of the ordinary." (TfA II 642)

Abstinence (*wara*ʿ)

Author: Abstinence of the *nafs* is renunciation of the world and the hereafter, while that of the heart is renunciation of everything other than God.

***

Tustarī: Abstinence means renouncing the *nafs* and with it the world. (TA 319)

Yaḥyā b. Muʿādh: Abstinence is of two kinds: the outward, which arises only when God inspires it; and the inward, which is such that only God enters your heart. (TA 371)

Qushayrī: Abstinence is to let go of whatever is not necessary for you. Ibrāhīm Adham said, "Abstinence is the letting go of suppositions and whatever is of no use to you, meaning abandonment of any excess." (RQ 166)

Thawrī: I have never seen anything easier than abstinence, because it lets go of everything the *nafs* desires. (RQ 168)

Shiblī: Abstinence is avoiding everything but God. (RQ 167)

Yaḥyā b. Muʿādh: Abstinence means sticking to the strictures of knowledge to its very limits without interpretation. (RQ 167)

Temptation (*waswasa*) and Inspiration (*ilhām*)

Murtaʿish: Temptation leads to bewilderment (*ḥayrat*), while inspiration leads to an increase in understanding and expression. (TSS 350)

Fidelity (*wafā*)

Author: Fidelity is keeping your pledge with your life.

***

Anṣārī: Seek fidelity from the authentic, for only authenticity does not commit error. (TGZ 663)

Shiblī: Fidelity is sincerity in speaking and an inner being steeped in veracity. (TSS 339)

Let's practice fidelity and incur
blame and be glad,
For on our Path it's unbelief
to take offense.

Ḥāfiẓ

The Moment (*waqt*)

Author: The moment is said to be the time in which you are present. In sufi terminology, the moment occurs in the state of meditation when you have no thought of past or future and you are even unaware of yourself.

***

Rūzbihān: The moment is between the past and the future in the time of meditation. The reality of it is the reception in the heart of subtleties from the Unseen. Junayd said, "When the precious moment disappears, one is unaware." (SS 548)

Junayd: Once the moment has flown, one can never receive it again. There is nothing more precious than the moment. (TA 444)

Junayd: The moment is an expression between two nothings which are partners in opposition. (QQ II 271)

Wāsiṭī: The finest devotional practice is the maintenance of the moment. This means not exceeding the limits, standing by God alone, and not going outside one's moment. (RQ 293)

Qaṣṣāb: Everyone is a prisoner of the moment, and the moment is God. Everyone is a prisoner of consciousness, and consciousness is God. (TA 643)

Abū ʿAbd Allāh Maghribī: The finest of actions is the tailoring of moments to conformity with God. (TSS 243)

Anonymous: The sufi is the child of the moment.

Qushayrī's commentary: Such a one is engaged in what is appropriate, being steadfast in doing in the moment what one has been directed to do. (RQ 89)

Ḥallāj (on being asked if the gnostic has a moment): No, because having a moment applies only to one who is qualified by 'being in the moment'. If someone takes comfort in his own qualities, he cannot be a gnostic.

ʿAṭṭār's commentary: The meaning of this is confirmed by the Prophetic Tradition: "I have a moment with God." (TA 588)

Anṣārī: The one-in-moment is the one whose moment is such that he has thought of neither the past nor the future. Thought of either involves loss of the moment. It has been said that the gnostic enjoys the purity of being the child of his moment. (TfA II 598)

Ad-Daqqāq: Your moment is where you are. If your moment is the world, you are in the world. If your moment is the hereafter, you are in the hereafter. If your moment is joy, you are in joy. If your moment is sorrow, you are in sorrow. (TA 656)

The Friend of God (*walī*) and Friendship with God (*walāyat*)

Author: The friend of God is one who is liberated from the ego and has become joined with God.

***

Abū ʿAlī Jawzjānī: The friend of God is one who is annihilated from his own state and subsistent in witnessing God. God is the Controller responsible for his actions, while he has no volition of his own and finds no peace in association with what is other than God. (TA 563)

Nasawī: Whoever displays his own miracles is a show-off, whereas whoever has miracles displayed through him by God is a friend of God. (TSA 490)

Bāyazīd: God is aware of what passes in the hearts of His friends. He has seen that some of them lack the ability to bear the burden of knowing Him, and so He has preoccupied them with worshipping Him. (TA 193)

Qushayrī: The friend of God (*walī*) has two meanings. One is that God is the Controller of his actions, not letting him return to himself for even a moment, while serving as his constant support and guide.

The other meaning is that he carries out his own devotional practice and worship of God. His practice is continuous and undinted by any transgression.

These two attributes are prerequisites for one to be a *walī*. It is incumbent on the *walī* to fully heed and observe God's requirements, while God maintains him through good and ill. (RQ 427)

Ibrāhīm Adham (to a man who wanted to be a friend of God): Desire not the slightest thing in the world nor in the hereafter. Occupy yourself with God, and disengage from your *nafs*. Finally, turn your attention to God, that He may accept you and make you His friend. (RQ 430)

Bāyazīd: God's friends are His brides, and brides are seen only by those allowed close access. Those who are close to God are hidden in the bridal chambers of intimacy, invisible in both the world and the hereafter. (RQ 431)

Aspiration (*himmat*)

Author: Aspiration means abandoning one's own existence for that of God.

***

Ibn ʿAṭāʾ: Aspiration is such that not a single outward occurrence can nullify it. (TA 493)

Shiblī: Aspiration means seeking God. Anything less than this is not aspiration. One with aspiration is preoccupied by nothing, while one with devotion is preoccupied. (TA 632)

Bāyazīd: The unbelief of those with aspiration is more flawless than the faith of those who rely on God's indulgence. (TSA 105)

Abū Bakr Ṭamistānī: The greatest aspiration is to emerge from the *nafs*, because the *nafs* is the greatest veil between you and God. (TSA 515)

Make my aspiration my escort
on the Path, O Sacred Bird,
for the way to the goal is long
and I'm a novice starting out.

Ḥāfiẓ

Identity (*huwiyyat*)

Rūzbihān: The *h* of God's *huwiyyat* is an indication, and God is beyond indication. (SS 535)

Rūzbihān: God protect us from dualism! Your identity lies in our non-identity. Between us there is a clash of ego-identities. So please remove our ego-identity! (SS 421)

Awe (*haybat*) and Intimacy (*uns*)

In terms of station, awe and intimacy are higher than contraction and expansion, just as contraction is higher than fear and expansion higher than hope. If awe is higher than contraction, intimacy is more complete than expansion. The reality of awe is absence; so every awestruck one is absent. There are different forms of awe, just as there are different forms of absence.

The reality of intimacy is sobriety in God, so that all intimate ones are sober. There are differences among the sober, just as there are different forms of imbibing. It is said that the lowest level of intimacy is where if you bring the intimate one into hell, his intimacy will not be darkened. (RQ 97)

Certitude (*yaqīn*)

Author: Certitude is the profession of a knowledge which comes with testimony of the heart.

***

Junayd: Certitude is the establishment of a knowledge in the heart which is not subject to change. (RQ 274)

Abū Saʿīd Kharrāz: Knowledge is that which leads you to act, while certitude is that which takes possession of you. (TA 462)

Abū Turāb [Nakhshabī]: I saw a youth walking in the desert without provision or mount. "If he lacks certitude in God," I thought to myself, "destruction will be the outcome." Then I said to the lad, "So you go about in a place like this without provision or steed?"

"Old man," he replied, "lift up your head! Do you see anyone but God?"

"Now," I said, "go where you will!" (RQ 276)

Ibn Khafīf: Certitude means the inner consciousness (*sirr*) becoming aware of the dictates of the Unseen. (RQ 272)

No more does Ḥāfiẓ enjoy
presence in class or retreat
than the learned scholar possesses
the knowledge of certitude.

Ḥāfiẓ

Every supposition
thirsts for certitude, my boy;
it increasingly
flaps and flaps its wings.

Mathnawī

List of Sources

Listed below are the abbreviations used in this book to refer to the classical Sufi texts from which certain passages in the book are quoted. The name of each text is set forth below opposite the corresponding abbreviation.

Each quoted prose passage in the book is followed by a citation, set forth in parantheses, indicating by the designated abbreviation the source of the quotation.

AAK *Aḥwāl u aqwāl-i Shaikh Abū l-Ḥasan Kharaqānī*
AM *ʿAwārif al- Maʿārif* (as-Suhrawardī)
AT *Asrār at-Tawḥīd* (Ibn Munawwar)
DNK *Dīwān-i Nāṣir-i Khusraw*
GR *Gulshan-i Rāz* (Shabistarī)
HH *Ḥadīqat al-Ḥaqīqat* (Sanā'ī)
HKh *Ḥikmat-i Khusrawānī* (Hāshim Raḍī)
HyA *Ḥilyat al-awliyā'* (Ḥafiẓ Abū Nuʿaym al-Iṣfahānī)
IU *Iḥyāʿ ʿulūm ad-dīn* (Abū Ḥāmid al-Ghazālī)
JK *Jāwīdān-i Khirad* (Miskawayh)
JNr *Junayd* (Nurbakhsh)
JTI *Justujū dar Taṣawwuf-i Īrān* (Zarrīnkūb)

KAd *Kawkab ad-Durrī* (Ibn ʿArabī)
KAM *Kashf al-Asrār* (Maybudī)
KM *Kashf al-maḥjūb* (Hujwīrī)
KST *Khulāṣa-yi Sharḥ-i Taʿarruf fī madhhab at-taṣawwuf* (Anon.)
LT *Kitāb al-Lumaʿ fi t-taṣawwuf* (al-Sarrāj)
MH *Misbāḥ al-hidāya* (ʿIzz ad-Dīn Maḥmūd Kāshānī)
MzH *Mazdayasnā wa ḥukūmat* (Sayyid Jalāl ad-Dīn Āshtiyānī)
NfU *Nafaḥāt al-uns* (Jāmī)
NKAT *an-Nūr min kalimāt Abī Ṭayfūr* (as-Sahlajī)
QQ *Qūt al-qulūb* (Abū Ṭālib al-Makkī)
RQ *Tarjuma-yi Risāla-yi Qushayriyya*
RSh *Rasā'il Shāh Niʿmatullāh Walī*
SkS *Silk as-sulūk* (Ḍiyāʾ ad-Dīn an-Nakhshabī)
SS *Sharh-i Shaṭḥiyyat* (Rūzbihān Baqlī)
ST *Sharh-i Taʿarruf* (Mustamlī)
TA *Tadhkirat al-awliyāʾ* (ʿAṭṭār)
TAQ *Tamhīdāt,* ʿAyn al-Quḍāt Hamadānī (ed. A. ʿUsayran)
TB *Tārīkh Baghdād* (al-Khaṭīb al Baghdādī)
TbA *Ṭabaqāt al-awliyāʾ* (Ibn Mulaqqin)
TbK *Ṭabaqāt al-Kubrā* (Shaʿrānī)
TfA *Tafsīr-i adabī wa ʿirfānī* (Khwāja ʿAbd Allāh Anṣārī)
TGZ *Tārīkh-i Guzīda* (Ḥamdullāh Mustawfī)
TH *Ṭarā'iq al-ḥaqā'iq* (Maʿṣūm ʿAlī Shāh Shīrāzī)
TSA *Ṭabaqāt aṣ-ṣūfiyya* (Khwāja ʿAbd Allāh Anṣārī)
TSS *Ṭabaqāt aṣ-ṣūfiyya* (as-Sulamī)

Index of Terms

Absolute Divinity 39
Abstinence 276
Adherence to Divine Unity and the Adherent to Divine Unity 88
Alienation 216
Allusion and Expression 38
Ambition 97
Annihilation and Subsistence 225
Ascetic Discipline 162
Asceticism and the Ascetic 163
Aspiration 281
Association 182
Audition and Ecstasy 167
Awe and Intimacy 283
Being and Nothingness 273
Cardinal Sins 233
Certitude 283
Chivalry 102
Claimant, The 243
Commanding Right and Forbidding Wrong 40
Concentration and Dispersion 99
Constancy 36
Contentment 158
Contentment-with-Sufficiency 231

Contraction and Expansion 229
Daily Prayers and Fasting 266
Deception 256
Detachment from the World 55
Determinism and Free Will 98
Devoteeship 48
Devotion 31
Devotional Practice 185
Disciple and the Master, The 247
Eternal Life 128
Ethics of the Sufis, The 25
Etiquette 30
Evil and the Ultimate Evil 170
Exegesis or Interpretation 77
Faith and Unbelief and Believer and Unbeliever 46
Favoring of Others 44
Fear 56
Fear and Hope 143
Festival 215
Fidelity 277
Fluctuation, Stability, Extinction and Effacement 82
Fortune 151
Freedom 120
Friend of God and Friendship with God, The 280
Generosity, Liberality and Meanness 109
Gnostic, The 189
Gnosis 252
God is Greater! 38
God or the Truth 123
God's Bestowal 198
God-cognition 131

Gossip 218
Greed 189
Guide or Master 33
Harmony 261
Heart, The 147
Heart-based Soul, The 161
Heart-discernment 220
Heaven and Hell 51
Humanity 246
Humility 85
Hypocrisy 161
"I am the Truth" 40
'I and You' 257
Identity 282
Idol, The 47
Incurring Blame 256
Intellect and the Reasoner 198
Intermediary, The 272
Intimacy 41
Intoxication and Sobriety 165
Jealousy-in-Love 219
Joy and Sorrow 169
Kindness towards Others 172
Knowledge and the Knower 209
Law, the Path and Reality, The 171
Litany 275
Litany on the Tongue and Remembrance in the Soul 275
Livelihood 239
Love 195
Loving-kindness and Friendship 237

Luminous Manifestation, Effulgence and Auroral Illumination 235
Lust 177
Magnification [of God's Name] 81
Making Accusations 97
Marriage 32
Meditation and Attention 243
Mercy 157
Moment, The 278
Muslim-ness and Muslim 248
Need 110
Need and Freedom from Need 269
Obligatory Practice and Customary Practice 223
One Who Has Reached Union, The 273
Oneness 274
Overwhelmings 217
Passing Thoughts 141
Patched Cloak and the Water-skin, The 244
Path of God, The 156
Patience 179
People 138
People on the Mystical Path to God, The 43
Perplexity and Bewilderment 129
Piety 80
Pilgrimage and Visitation of the Ka'ba, The 112
Polytheist, The 251
Poverty and the Pauper 223
Practice of Poverty 54
Preacher, The 177
Presence and Absence 121
Pride 234

Reason and Love 199
Recognition of the Divine Unity of Being 174
Reflection 78
Remembrance 151
Repentance 85
Reprisal 208
Retreat and Seclusion 139
Savor and Imbibing 154
Seclusion 195
Seeking Forgiveness 36
Seeking the Way and Seeking God 187
Seeking, Finding and Witnessing 187
Self, The 262
Service 133
Shame 128
Silence 129
Sincerity 23
Singularity 222
Ṣirāṭ Bridge, The 184
Staring at Others 48
State and Station 111
Submission 37
Submissiveness 135
Sufis' Clothing, The 235
Sufism, the Sufi, the Sufiologist, the Dervish and Dervishness 56
Supplicatory Prayer 145
Temperament 136
Temptation and Inspiration 277
Thanks 173
Transgression 255

Trust-in-God, Submission and Consignment 93
Truth and Falsity 125
Unity of God and the Unity of Creation, The 93
Unity, its Affirmer and the Object of Affirmation 92
Veil 119
Veracity 183
Vision of Certitude, the Knowledge of Certitude and the Truth of Certitude, The 215
Wisdom 126
Witnessing, Visionary Revelation and Presential Vision 249
World and the Hereafter, The 148
Worship and the Worshipper 194
Worst of Times, The 48
Would-be Ecstasy, Ecstasy and True Being 83
Yearning 176

Nimatullahi Sufi Order Centers

United States

306 West 11th Street
New York, New York 10014
U.S.A.
Tel: 212-924-7739

4931 MacArthur Blvd. NW
Washington, D.C. 20007
U.S.A.
Tel: 202-338-4757

84 Pembroke Street
Boston, Massachusetts 02118
U.S.A.
Tel: 617-536-0076

4021 19th Avenue
San Francisco, California 94132
U.S.A.
Tel: 415-586-1313

11019 Arleta Avenue
Mission Hills, Los Angeles,
California 91345, U.S.A.
Tel: 818-365-2226

219 Chace Street
Santa Cruz, California 95060
U.S.A.
Tel: 831-425-8454

310 NE 57th Street
Seattle, Washington 98105
U.S.A.
Tel: 206-527-5018

4642 North Hermitage
Chicago, Illinois 60640
U.S.A.
Tel: 773-561-1616

405 Greg Avenue
Santa Fe, New Mexico 87501
U.S.A.
Tel: 505-983-8500

3018 Felicita Road
Escondido, San Diego,
California 92029, U.S.A.
Tel: 760-489-7834

656 Emily Drive
Mountain View, California 94043
U.S.A.
Tel: 650-960-3429

Canada

1596 Ouest avenue des Pins
Montreal H3G 1B4
Quebec, Canada
Tel: 514-989-1411

1784 Lawrence Avenue West
North York, Toronto,
Ontario M6L 1E2
Canada
Tel: 416-242-9397

1735 Mathers Avenue
West Vancouver, B.C.
V7V 2G6 Canada
Tel: 604-913-1144

Mexico

Miguel Angel Garcia #49
La Lejona, segunda seccion
San Miguel de Allende
C.P. 37765
Guanajuato, Mexico
Tel: 52-415-120-21-55

Europe

41 Chepstow Place
London W2 4TS
England
Tel: 020-7229-0769

95 Old Lansdowne Road
West Didsbury, Manchester
M20 2NZ, England
Tel: 0161-434-8857

Kölnerstraße 176
51149 Köln
Germany
Tel: 49 220-315-390

50 rue du Quatrième Zouaves
Rosny-sous-Bois 93110
Paris, France
Tel: 331-485 52809

116, avenue Charles de Gaulle
69160 Tassin-La-Demi-Lune
Lyon, France
Tel: 478-342-016

C/Abedul 11
Madrid 28036
Spain
Tel: 3491-350-2086

Cabezas, 9
14003 Córdoba
Spain
Tel: 957-48-4391

Ringvägen 5
17276 Sundbyberg
Sweden
Tel: 46-8983-767

Jan van Goyenkade 19
2311 BA, Leiden
The Netherlands
Tel: 31-71-5124001

Getreidemarkt 3 /1A-1060
Wien, Austria
Tel: 431-9414022

Number II, House 4
Building 1A, Devyatkin Pereulok
Moscow, Russia
Tel: 7095-9247000

House 4, Building 43-H
1-2 Floors, Kapitanskaya Street
St. Petersburg, Russia
Tel: 921-0906611

Africa

63 Boulevard Latrille
BP 1224 Abidjan
CIDEX , 1 Côte d'Ivoire
Tel: 225-22410510

Quartier Beaurivage
BP 1599 Porto-Novo, Bénin
Tel: 229-20-214706

Azimmo Secteur 16
Villa 12, Ouaga 2000
10 BP 356
Ouagadougou, Burkina Faso
Tel: 226-50-385797

Quartier Guema
02 BP 86
Parakou, Bénin

Liberté VI extension, Lot # 1
Croisement Rues CY 113 et GY94
P.O. Box 5871
Dakar Fann, Sénégal
Tel: 221-33-867-3869

Australia

87A Mullens Street
Balmain 2041,
Sydney, Australia
Tel: 612-9555-7546